Mom, Y

Jenny Dean Schmidt

Mom, You're Amazing

Changing The World
One Life at a Time

Jenny Dean Schmidt

ISBN: 978-0-9840385-6-5

This book is available at special quantity discounts for sales promotions, premiums, fund-raising and educational needs. Special books or book excerpts also can be created to fit specific needs. For inquiries, contact us at:

SpSales@PeaksPublishing.com

Published by Peaks Publishing Inc
Printed in the United States of America

Cover Design: 100Covers

Praise for *Mom, You're Amazing*

"Jenny has written a book that you'll want to revisit each year for an annual pep talk."
- Mandi Arioto, CEO, Mothers of Preschoolers International (MOPS)

"If you feel overlooked, unappreciated and unimportant as a mom, this book is for you. Jenny helps you see how much you matter, what a difference you are making in this world. Heaven misses nothing you do with love. You are amazing!"
- Sheila Walsh, host of *Life Today*

"This book is the motivation you need for your motherhood. Jenny shares dramatic stories to remind moms of their immeasurable importance while revealing eight secrets to help moms be all they can be."
- Dr. Emerson Eggerichs, author of *Love & Respect*

"Jenny is a virtual cheerleader for moms. Not only does she offer the ultimate mom pep talk, but she shares mothering secrets that will take your mom game to the next level."
- Dr Kevin Leman, New York Times bestselling author of *Have a New Kid By Friday*, *Sheet Music* and *The Birth Order Book*

"This book just might be the most rewarding message a mom could read this year. Just reading it could transform your motherhood."
- Tonya Milligan, author, *No Perfect Parent, Just a Perfect Purpose*

"This book is like a Mother's Day card on steroids! This collection of personal insights and mothering "secrets" will power moms through the messiness of motherhood to the true joy that mothering can be as they experience this life-changing encouragement and inspiration."
  - Jami Kirkbride LPC, Co-author of *The You Zoo* and founder of
    Parenting With Personality

"I was raised by a single mom and know how hard it can be. Jenny helps you see your rock star status and mega influence as a mom."
  - Matt Paxton, former Host of *Hoarders*

"As a professional coach who empowers the authentic potential in women, I know encouragement when I see it. This book will lift your heart and remind you of the significant meaning in your mothering."
  - Dale Wilsher, Author of *What's Your Mom Type?*

DEDICATION

To the One
who created all mothers,
all fathers,
and all children.

To the father
of our own two children,
my husband, Mike.

To the children
who made my motherhood happen,
Otis and Georgia Grace.

To the parents
who brought me into this world.

I love you.

Acknowledgements

Can you put Almighty God in the acknowledgments? Because I must thank Him for giving me this book, from start to finish. Thank You, Lord.

Then, I must thank my tireless, brilliant and risk-taking publishers, Tom and Lindy Schneider of Peaks Publishing, who gave me the gift of gracious encouragement and believed in the message of this book wholeheartedly.

I thank the consummate "connector," Jennifer, for bringing Tom and Lindy into my life.

I probably cannot thank my mom and dad enough. My dad passed along his DNA with the ability to write and the courage to do so. My mom, the one who exists to help improve everyone else's life, generously committed herself to endless hours of editing and re-editing. I would sometimes dread the latest round of mom's "red pen" edits, but she was almost always right.

Here's where I thank my brother just for being, well, my brother.

And I am ever so grateful to my executive assistant, Michele, who I call the "best assistant ever." She is also an incredible copy editor—eagle eyes for errors.

I am truly grateful to ChannelMom's Board of Directors, for encouraging me and praying for me through the nearly seven-year process of writing and completing this book.

Also grateful for my faithful friends (from far and near) who have cheered me on so sweetly from the sidelines— including my BFF, Shel, and also Kathy, Katy, and Kori—who prompted me to write this book in the first place.

My thanks also goes out to my savvy PR friend, Jeane, who encouraged me while giving me the hard truths about publishing.

Of course, I must express my gratitude to the seven wonderful women who shared their brutal and beautiful stories for the benefit of other moms—Yvonne, Shelly, Linda, Gretchen, Michele, Mari and Kara.

I am also deeply appreciative of my compatriot in the work of championing the sacred office of "mom," CEO of MOPS, Mandy Arioto.

Finally, more thanks than I can express to my steady, supportive and sacrificing husband, Mike, and to my most precious and loving children, Otis and Georgia Grace—there would be no mom behind this book without them.

Free Resource
Productive Parenting Calendar

As a mom, sometimes you're just too tired to find teachable moments and pass on crucial life lessons. That's where the Productive Parenting Calendar comes in! This handy, little year-long calendar offers 52 easy-to-use ideas for passing on great life lessons to your kids while sparking their creativity and improving their attitude!

Each weekly activity brings out the fun in both parent and child while teaching character, compassion and creativity. They are great for family bonding time.

**Get your FREE
Productive Parenting Calendar at**

MomYoureAmazing.com/calendar

Table of Contents

FOREWORD

Moms are the fiercest, most powerful creatures on the planet, evidenced by the fact that the word "mother" describes formidable things—like a mother bear or the mother of all storms. However, even though moms are fiercely raising the next generation, the work of motherhood often goes unnoticed and unappreciated. That's why it is my unique privilege, as the CEO of MOPS (Mothers of Preschoolers) International, to lead an organization that supports moms all over the world. It's also why I am so passionate about this book. *"Mom, You're Amazing"* unabashedly cheers moms on, as they embark on the most significant and influential work they will ever do.

Jenny Dean Schmidt is a friend, but she is also someone I look up to. She is brilliant, kind, and a gifted communicator—watching her host her radio show is mesmerizing. Her vulnerability, combined with her ability to talk about the tough stuff, is unmatched. Jenny is the real deal. A trusted confidant whose words have challenged me to view motherhood with a fresh perspective, and I am guessing will do the same for you.

Jenny begins the book by sharing her own captivating story to help us understand why she has a never-say-die commitment to moms and motherhood. Then, using her training as a former reporter, Jenny uncovers the riveting stories of seven uniquely amazing moms. Moms who have faced struggles, setbacks, and suffering, and have now come out on the other side to share crucial mothering lessons with us.

There's the mom who forgave the unforgivable. We find ourselves perched with a bird's eye view of this mom's tragedy but privy to a close-up of her emotional journey from faith to forgiveness. The journey takes her (and us) into prison cells, courtrooms, and even to the set of *Oprah*, as this tenacious mother seeks to find a killer and secure justice.

We're invited into the drama of a mother whose son became famous overnight but suffered the cost of fame. We see what it is like to be the "mom" behind an overexposed contestant on the TV spectacle known as *The Bachelorette*. This mama's "Amazing Mom Secret" is a life-saving approach to 21st century digital dangers and social media mayhem faced by almost every parent.

Then we meet the mom who raised 106 children (105 wasn't enough?). This mom exposes a foster care system bursting at the seams and the underbelly of the "family breakdown" in America. Her personal stories of fostering carry the potential to shock you and motivate you. We learn about the things that usually hide behind family dysfunction and how we can choose to overcome them. The secret shared by this mother-of-many will remind you to focus on what matters most.

Next is the mom whose face may be familiar to you. You've seen her on TV, on movie screens, and on the Miss America stage. This mom was one of the forerunners in the #MeToo movement, as she blazed a trail seeking justice for workplace sexual harassment. Her life story was turned into an Oscar-nominated movie, but that didn't get in the way of her continued commitment to her husband and kids. This woman single-handedly proves that a mom can pursue both career and motherhood simultaneously and successfully. Still, she admits that moms have their limits, and her secret is a reminder that no mom should succumb to the pressure to "have it all."

We also hear from the mom who overcame cancer three times and adopted three kids in the middle of it. Her cancer almost took her life, her family, and her career. But this mama has more fight than even she knew. Her trials surpass most, but her strength is an inspiration. This mom's secret provides us with gentle marching orders for raising our babies well.

Then we meet the mom who is a Latin singing sensation, despite unimaginable abuse that threatened to snuff out her voice. The singer shares her incredible journey from abuse at her mother's hands to the healing that occurred when she entered motherhood herself. Influenced by her unwavering faith and stand-in family, her secret will be a comfort to any mom with a difficult past.

Finally, we get an intimate peek into the life and death of a brave mama who was the subject of a popular documentary. This incredible mother shared her story on-camera while she was dying—gracefully teaching us all how to say "goodbye" with the hope of Heaven. Her story is an appropriate finish for this collection of Amazing Moms, because she inspires us to commit to the most important thing. Love.

Jenny has written a book that you'll want to revisit each year for an annual pep talk. It's a moving manifesto that gives dignity and depth to the holy work of mothering. I can't wait for you to dive in.

- Mandy Arioto
President and CEO, MOPS International

READ THIS PREFACE. IT MATTERS.

I recently accompanied our teenage daughter to a boy-band concert. I was mildly horrified at the thought of being the oldest person in the audience. As it turned out, other "old" parents were there too. Maybe those parents were trying to keep their teens inside the same protective bubble wrap I've kept my kids in for years.

As I watched the adulating arms in the audience— worshipping the band members with one hand and holding their phones in the other—I thought to myself, who raised these babies? What unseen moms are behind these happy, young faces? I wondered this because the kids in that audience, most of them, owe much of their existence to the moms who got them this far.

****

At the moment I begin this book, I am typing with my pajamas on. My hair is unbrushed. My glasses are smudged. Yesterday's mascara is now under my eyes. I have two drinking containers on my desk and an empty cereal bowl on the floor. One child sleeps in the room to my left, the other in the room to my right. The desk where I work sits in a hallway cubby between my children's bedrooms. The crock pot still languishes in the kitchen, displaying the remains of last night's dinner. It's almost noon on a Saturday.

There's something very typical about my Saturday state of affairs. Most moms can identify with the messy consequences of putting their kids before their own needs. They're familiar with the thankless nature of sacrifice for the love of a child. And, no, I'm not just talking about stay-at-home moms or homeschooling moms or holier-than-thou moms.

I'm talking about *every* kind of mom. This book is for every woman who has ever mothered, whatever her shape, size, color, background or neighborhood. From the first to the last mom featured in these pages, the focus is on the amazing value of moms. Whether you've been a mom for biological children, adopted children, foster children, grandchildren—or anyone else you've found to mother—this book is for you.

My passion is to help each mom realize her incredible importance. The importance of her position as a mom. I think we forget how BIG a mother's job is. Moms have been charged with raising the next generation. If they do it well, the world benefits. If they do it poorly, the world suffers. Darrow L. Miller once wrote, "The death of motherhood leads very quickly to the death of nations." Yet how often do nations recognize that moms hold them together? And how often does the world thank moms for children well-raised? Maybe once a year. On Mother's Day.

Perhaps you're a mom who feels overwhelmed, under-appreciated and undervalued by our world. Author Julie Roys says that, instead of undervaluing motherhood, we should "seek to restore motherhood in the eyes of the culture... promoting it as an essential component of a flourishing society, as well as a high spiritual calling."

I love how Roys extols the value of moms. I don't think we value motherhood enough. Oh, our culture pays lip service to the idea of "mom and apple pie," but it hardly ever broadcasts the virtues of motherhood. In fact, our societal oversight probably gave birth to the common phrase, "I'm *just* a mom."

But, oh, my dear mom, you are SO much more than "just." Allow me to prove it to you. You're about to get a front row seat as fellow moms reveal the secrets behind their amazing-ness. You'll discover how they feel like you, struggle like you, cry like you and laugh like you. And they'll prove that every mom can find multiple ways to be amazing for her kids.

I've chosen to feature seven very different moms. Each has an incredible story and an unforgettable secret of good mothering.

My own mothering opinions pop up in my conversations with these moms. I try to share my opinions with grace, because I don't want one sentence of this book to make you feel judged or "less than." I simply want you to see the indispensable value of your mothering role—the care of the Creator applied through the hands and hearts of moms. By the end of the book, I hope you see yourself as a holy vessel on a critical mission of raising the next generation.

In the end, I've written this book because *the story of a mom is important.* Not one of the moms I portray is perfect. They'd all admit their flaws. In fact, the well-known son of one mom said his mother taught him that "we didn't have to be perfect. She knew she wasn't perfect. It was learn as you go. It was more that she showed us that she wasn't perfect and that allowed us to grow instead of trying to be something that isn't possible. I mean, you can't be perfect."

Beyond their imperfections, each of the moms in this book has a special mothering secret to pass along to you. My prayer is that God will cause the secrets and stories from these seven moms to uplift you, invigorate you, instruct you, inspire you, and motivate you in your daily walk as a mom. And may you come to know that you're amazing, because you're changing the world one life at a time.

CHAPTER 1
Embracing Motherhood
Jenny Dean Schmidt

On the day of the school shooting, I wasn't sure if my husband would live. On the day I was diagnosed with breast cancer, I didn't know if I would pull through. And on that life-changing day when our first child was born, I wasn't sure if I could be a good mom.

****

I guess I'll go first, but certainly not because my story is more important than the seven moms who follow me. Their lives are noteworthy. Their stories are incredible. I believe their stories will encourage you in your mothering story. Honestly, I'm not sure my mom credentials compare to theirs, but if "love of the job" is a credential, then I most definitely qualify. I love being "mom." I love that role in my own life. And I love it in the lives of billions of women who have carried the mothering banner throughout history.

I believe with all my heart that the sacrifice of motherhood is beautiful. I love the evolving beauty of being a mom. I find infinite delight in raising children. I treasure— from here to eternity—the babies that I birthed. I love them. I hold them. I teach them. I scold them. I would die for my children.

But I didn't always feel this way.

****

I wasn't really someone who made big plans to become a mother. As a young girl, I aspired to be "somebody," to make my mark in the world. Having babies was not necessarily part of that plan.

I grew up in an educated, intellectual, middle-class family in the Midwest. I had dedicated parents and a stable home life. I did well in school but decided not to pursue the academic life of my family. I wanted to be pretty and popular. I wanted to be approved of and admired. During childhood, I had two very specific goals: 1) to marry my nursery school sweetheart and 2) to become a TV reporter.

When I grew up, I did both.

I guess I was a fairly ambitious kid. I actually began to prepare myself for a television career while I was still in high school. I worked as a DJ for my small-town radio station and then interned at a cable TV station near my home. In college, I worked for a television production company in Hollywood, writing script snippets for the former wife of late-night TV host, Johnny Carson. Near the end of my college days, I designed an international fellowship that would allow me to work as an intern for BBC Television in London. BBC initially declined my naive proposal, but then a kindhearted producer from somewhere in the bowels of a gargantuan BBC building came across my written request for an internship. He somehow convinced somebody they should give me a shot.

I packed my bags and set out for London. All. By. Myself. I wasn't part of a program. I wasn't an exchange student. I didn't have a host family. I just landed at Heathrow Airport with approximately seven suitcases, looking like a clueless American. I moved into a little flat with a divorced mom from Poland and her pre-teen daughter. I walked into BBC with an optimistic vision of being put to work in their prestigious documentary department and then writing my senior thesis about my experience.

In retrospect, I'm not sure they really knew what to do with me. I think I was later told that I was the only American intern at BBC ever. In the end, I learned a lot about how the world-renowned broadcasting giant worked. I conducted interviews. I watched the production process. I even worked at a special anti-drug event that featured Princess Diana and had the privilege of saying "hi" to the beautiful, shy icon.

My internship at BBC paved the way for me to land a job at ABC News in Washington D.C. almost immediately after I graduated from college. I worked at ABC during the Reagan years and near the end of the Cold War. After my years at

ABC, I moved on to a stint as an associate producer for the MacNeil/Lehrer Newshour on PBS, also in D.C.

The demands of working in TV news in the bustling D.C. market eventually had me pining for something more familiar. And familiar had a name. Michael Allen Schmidt. Mike had been my sweetheart from nursery school through college. During our long courtship, we'd broken up approximately twenty-two times (not kidding)! After I made a long-distance move to rekindle our relationship, Mike and I finally married in 1989 in my parents' backyard in Minnesota. At our pre-nuptial meeting with the minister, we told him we did not expect to have children. Oh, how things change.

After getting married, I continued to pursue my career in television, which honestly had become my newfound "religion." I secured my first job as an on-air television reporter in southern California. Achieving my childhood dream of reporting the news on TV made me an idol, though mostly to myself. I came to find my meaning, my identity, my purpose and my self-worth from being on a screen that implied success.

My broadcast career would end up putting me in the employ of five different TV networks at stations across the nation. During that time, I had the privilege of interviewing history-makers and world-changers. I had a sit-down interview with former U.S. president Gerald Ford and questioned president-to-be Bill Clinton at a pre-campaign press conference.

I also interviewed a wide array of celebrities from the 80s and 90s, including Priscilla Presley, Hulk Hogan, Orel Hershiser, ZZ Top and Sonny Bono.

Oddly enough, I ended up developing a friendship with Sonny and his fourth wife, Mary. It happened in the years I reported at the NBC TV affiliate in Palm Springs, California. Although Sonny had experienced stratospheric fame during the days of The Sonny and Cher Show, he'd managed to remain humble. In fact, he was quick to talk about how rapidly "famous" can turn into "forgotten" and celebrity can turn sour. Sonny knew this from very personal experience, as he learned to be good-humored about being the butt of jokes in his guest appearances on TV shows like "*The Love Boat.*"

This former superstar had come to realize the fleeting and false nature of fame. It had turned on him and left him humbled. It was actually his humility that made Sonny a joy to be around. He was authentic and gracious. As mayor of Palm Springs and then congressman from that same district, he truly seemed to enjoy serving people.

A perfect illustration of Sonny's authentic generosity came on the day he met my mother-in-law. My husband's mom had come to visit us in Palm Springs. We'd made plans to take her to meet Sonny at a restaurant he owned in the area. My husband and I both hoped she'd be giddy over the opportunity to meet Mr. Bono and have something to tell her friends back in Minnesota.

Upon arriving at the restaurant, we were disappointed to learn that Sonny had gone home for the evening. Somehow, one of the staff got word to him that we were hoping we could give my mother-in-law the thrill of an introduction. So, Sonny left his house and came back to the restaurant to humor one middle-aged mother from Minnesota. He made a big fuss over her, asking her questions about her life in the Midwest and making her feel like she was the celebrity, not him.

****

Celebrities were just a small part of my reporting days. I also interviewed politicians and pundits and world leaders. Getting access to historical figures and being paid to report on historical events were perks of the job. Sometimes I feel like I've lived a Forrest Gump kind of life because I've come face-to-face with so many history-makers and history-making-events over the years.

I loved those perks and I cherished my career. But I was also ashamed of it. I was ashamed of the fact that TV news is the epitome of our culture glamorizing the wrong things for the wrong reasons.

Overall, broadcast news deserves its bad reputation. Good journalism is often sacrificed in favor of sensationalism. This formula creates a "vulture" mentality in the news business. I witnessed multiple examples of vulture journalism during my fifteen years in TV.

One incident involved a fire in a small-town store in Ohio. The store stocked gunpowder, so the fire quickly became explosive. Our newsroom kept getting updates on the number of people injured or killed in the explosions. At one point, when we were given the latest body count, I remember a news staffer reading the copy and yelling to one of the anchors, "Oh, it's getting better and better! Now there are three dead and two of them are kids!"

On another "birds-of-prey" news day, our newsroom got reports of a window-washer falling to his death from a high-rise. I remember one of the producers reacting with a little celebration, not hiding her merriment over the fact that she now had "a great lead" for that evening's news.

TV news can be a nasty business as news personalities make their living off of other people's tragedies. But there's a more subtle tragedy going on behind the scenes. Viewers may detest the media for what it portrays on their screens, but they also glorify media personalities because they happen to be on those screens. It's ironic. These personalities, with their perfectly coiffed hair and made-up faces, get honored for spewing news about murders, car wrecks, scandals and tragedies of the day.

I discovered, personally, how the public honors people whose faces adorn their screens, through the special treatment I received when I was a reporter. In some ways, I lived the glamorous life of a famous person. Of course, I wasn't on the level of media superstars, but people treated me as a local celebrity, asking for my autograph and offering me free dinners.

Unfortunately, I bought into this special attention. I allowed it to deceive me into thinking I was more important than other people just because I happened to be on TV.

****

It wasn't until I became a mom that I realized how I'd been seduced by the celebrity treatment I received as a TV broadcaster. It became clear to me that our culture glorifies people who are visible. These glorified folks are not necessarily honored because they're contributing great things to our world. They're honored because they're recognizable. Our pop culture makes a big deal over people like the Kardashians—just because of their public personas— the famous honored for being famous.
Nothing more.

We don't idolize the nameless people who feed the hungry or tend to the sick; instead, we worship people who make touchdowns or Tik Tok videos. Our children are told that success means becoming major league ball players or supermodels, potentially demeaning millions of kids who won't become those things. As our kids prepare for adulthood, society tells them it's more important to be in the NFL than to be a good neighbor... or it's better to be on the cover of *People* than to help people in need... or that earning tons of cash is superior to rearing a child with a lot less cash!

When being "rich and famous" is our biggest ideal, we're often overlooking the folks who give the most to our world. People like moms. People like dads. People who are shaping the future of our world by the way in which they raise their children. Are celebrities celebrated because they're making the world a better place? Usually not. More likely, it's for their latest movie or Academy Award.

> *We're often overlooking the folks who give the most to our world. People like moms.*

My point is not to bash celebrities. I'm simply pointing out what we're up against as moms. Being a mother has never been a path to fame and fortune, but in the twenty-first century, moms are bombarded by millions of messages from cyberspace, television, radio, movies, magazines, iPads and iPhones—messages that suggest we moms are nobodies. We're told that what we do as moms is not really important or noteworthy. That is why it has become my mission to help moms like you see the amazing value of your mothering, no matter what our culture is saying to you.

Allow me to use an illustration to prove my point about your mom role being sacred. During my time in television, I won an Emmy award for my political reporting. Over the years, I have used my Emmy as a prop when giving speeches to various mom groups. I ask the moms in the audience to compare two events that I reenact in front of them. First, I throw down "a red carpet" (a red towel) and ask the moms to clap for me as I walk down that red carpet with my Emmy award hoisted in the air. They kindly give me a round of gracious applause. Then I put my Emmy away and kneel down on the red carpet (which, conveniently, has become a towel again). I invite one mom from the audience to sit in a chair next to the towel. I then place this mom's feet into a tub of warm water and I gently wash them, toes, heels and all.

After I complete these two exercises (and give the mom the red towel for her feet), I ask the women in the audience a few questions. I inquire, "which of those two events, walking the red carpet or washing the feet, would the world say is more important?" They answer, "walking the red carpet." Then I ask, "which one of these tasks is a mom more likely to do?" They know this. They say, "wash feet." And finally, I ask, "which one of these tasks did Jesus ask us to do?" The answer is obvious. And this is just one more proof that a mom's work, even when it seems mundane, is sacred.

****

One reason I feel strongly about helping moms see their ultimate value is that I had to do it for myself. Like many American women, I thought I was supposed to aim for that "celebrity" ideal. As I strived for that image, I began to believe that what made me most valuable was my hair... my face... my body... my sex appeal... my dress size (oh for goodness' sake!) and also having a successful career in television. I leaned into all of these things for my sense of self-worth and personal identity.

And then came motherhood. Out of the blue. Ticking clock, I guess. I suddenly decided that I very much wanted to be a mom. I was about 32 and working at the ABC affiliate in Cleveland. When I told my husband about my baby fever, he was mildly shocked. As it turned out, it wasn't as easy as "wanting" to be a mom. It took us a while. Doctors decided we needed to be put on a regimen for dealing with infertility. We went with the more affordable infertility treatments for several months. The third month was supposed to be the final try and we'd been told that our chances didn't look good.

After that third month, I remember taking the pregnancy test and being overjoyed. I think I planned some corny "reveal" to let my husband know our good news. Nearly nine months later, our baby boy arrived in a difficult birth. I had been in labor (with very slow progress) for almost two days when we finally went to the hospital on a Sunday morning. By this time, I was feeling exhausted; however, I told my husband and my doula that I did NOT want to have an epidural. I wanted to give birth naturally.

Hours after arriving at the hospital and after over an hour of pushing, one of the nurses said something like "uh oh." The nurse had just discovered that our baby was covered in meconium (the baby's stool within the placenta). In addition to that life-threatening issue, his pulse was dropping rapidly because the umbilical cord was wrapped around his neck.

They announced a "code yellow" over the speaker and the medical staff sprang into action. My doula and my husband told me that I HAD TO PUSH as hard as I could. They said this because they knew an emergency C-section would be my next option and that could have been dangerous for both me and our baby.

In that must-push moment, I remember thinking that I was so exhausted I could hardly imagine lifting my head, let alone pushing. But, with my husband quietly holding me, I pushed with all the might I could muster in those tension-filled seconds. By the grace of God, it was enough. Our baby was born, but he was in jeopardy. The room fell eerily quiet as doctors and nurses worked to suck meconium out of our baby's mouth and throat to make sure it didn't get into his lungs and compromise his breathing. I don't think they gave him that little hit on the back that prompted him to breathe until they were all done clearing him out. The only noise in the room was the sucking sound of the vacuum. We waited. And waited. And then our baby boy cried. For the first time.

We cried too. Our first child had arrived and we were overwhelmed. So. Incredibly. Grateful. We named him Otis Dean Schmidt. I remember holding him in the hospital room, carefully inspecting his little limbs and hands and feet, realizing that I had never loved anything more than him. The love a mother has for her child simply cannot be measured.

Just months after becoming a mom, I lost my prized job in television. A newly hired news director made the decision not to renew my contract. At the time, I considered my job loss a devastating blow. I faced a very tough transition from being labeled "important" as a TV broadcaster to being "not important" as a mom.

The world had offered me accolades for my position and my prestige. For years I'd received compliments for things like my clothes, my voice and how I looked on TV. But my mothering? People weren't rushing up to tell me what a fine mother I was. They weren't complimenting me for my commitment to raising my child well. Certainly, nobody was asking me for my autograph. "Oh, wow, you're a MOM. Can I have your autograph?!" That didn't happen. Truth be told, if a mom had to wait on other people's affirmation in order to know her worth, she'd have to wait a very long time.

Letting my media identity go and gaining a new identity for myself—as a wife, a mother and, eventually, as a child of God—was very difficult for me. Do you know, there are people in my little town who lost interest in talking to me once they found out I was no longer on TV? To them, I wasn't important anymore.

I find a kindred spirit in the writings of Julie Roys, who also believes our culture doesn't respect the role of motherhood. Roys suggests we should be cheering on moms, reminding them that "even in its most reduced form, **motherhood is one of the most crucial roles in all of culture.** The family is the fundamental building block of society, so nurturing the next generation is essential if societies are to thrive."

I began to realize, ever so slowly, the value that God saw in my motherhood.

When I entered motherhood, I longed (almost daily) for that old sense of TV self-worth. I held fast to the idea that my television job mattered more than my mom job. I would even introduce myself to people like this: "Well, I used to be a TV reporter, but now I'm a stay-at-home mom." Yikes! Happily, that pathetic introduction eventually faded away as I adopted a different value system. I began to realize, ever so slowly, the value that God saw in my motherhood. It was a gradual transformation that unfolded over the first several years of my being mom to Otis.

But before my transformation, I had to face the upside-down realities of losing my job, my identity and my sense of significance. The loss of those "big" things caused me to spiral into a debilitating postpartum depression. And it was classic. I saw more dark than light. I could no longer see the point of it all. I'd look at my baby and think morbid thoughts like, "He's just going to die one day, and I'm going to die before he does." Life seemed futile. I struggled daily with thoughts of pointlessness and hopelessness.

I felt bad.

Fortunately, I did not feel bad about my baby. I was able to nurse him, hold him, coo over him and care for him (I'm aware that postpartum sometimes disables moms' emotions in a way that makes it hard for them to nurture and love). I loved our baby more than I'd known I was capable of loving anyone. However, I still felt sad. To top it off, I felt bad about feeling sad... especially as a new mama with a healthy baby.

When my depression started, I began to seek hope in a variety of "gods." Desperate to find anything to light up my dark perspective, I sought out seers and Googled gurus. I consulted spiritualists and searched for sages. I even attended a seminar on hearing angelic voices. Then, in the midst of my search, I stumbled upon the God of the Bible. Unexpectedly.

We had moved west from Cleveland to a little mountain town outside Denver. I'd taken a part-time job at a TV station in the Mile High City, so I split my time between the reporting job and my other job as part-time, stay-at-home mom.

Unfortunately, the move to "mile-high living" failed to lift my spirits a mile high. The struggle with depression plagued me. I began to pray regularly, asking my vague image of God to help me climb out of the dark pit. Maybe as an answer to my prayers, an acquaintance invited me to a Bible study. I began reading scripture regularly and I scoured the ancient text for answers, for a way—any way—to get beyond the darkness.

Then one day I decided I needed to "get over myself," in order to find what I was looking for. I thought I'd change my perspective with a day of volunteering at a Special Olympics event. I figured if those smiling competitors couldn't cheer me up, nothing could. But they did not bring me cheer. In fact, I recall walking around a little garden that was near the event with my son in a stroller telling God I couldn't take much more. I was losing my desire to stay alive.

After that dark declaration, I dropped by my parents' home in Denver. Neither my mom nor my dad were there at the time. I remember going into their master bathroom, falling down on the floor and crying out to God. I recall thinking something like, "I don't care if my intellectual family thinks it's stupid to call on Jesus. I'm going to do it anyway." I uttered this plea, "Jesus, will you please save me?"

After that simple prayer, I got up and took my baby back to our home in the foothills. The house was getting dark. I turned on some lights and headed to the bedroom to change Otis's diaper. I remember turning the radio on to a random station to provide some background music. I did not consider myself a Christian in those days, so I didn't purposely listen to Christian music.

As I began changing my baby boy, he reached out to hug my neck. I recall being surprised by his hug during a diaper change. I thought, "This is weird. He's never done this before." But I leaned down, accepted his little hug and then quickly stood up. (With baby boys, a mom likes to avoid being in firing range.) As I went on changing him, he insisted on pulling me down and giving me hugs. About the fourth or fifth time he reached up to hug me, I remember thinking, "This is so strange. His tiny face has the wisdom of a man, and he's so insistent that I must LET HIM HUG ME." I can't explain it fully, except to say that it seemed like he knew he was supposed to hold me. His beckoning arms and dogged insistence were pretty powerful for a one-and-a-half-year-old baby.

I finally decided to let my baby boy take me in his arms and hold me as long and as tightly as he wished. I lay my head on his chest and quietly rested there in the stillness of his body. He hugged me very close.

Slowly, I began to listen to the music on the radio, and a realization began to sweep over me. The song on the radio was "What a Friend We Have in Jesus." The lyrics state, "In His arms He'll take and shield thee. Thou wilt find a solace there." And that is exactly what my baby boy was doing for me—holding me in his arms, offering me solace, as the song gently spoke to my heart.

In that moment, I knew something as I'd never known anything before. I stood up and thought, "If I don't believe it tomorrow, I believe it today." I knew—through the hug of my son and through the lyrics of that song—that Jesus Himself had answered my prayer. Much like two thousand years ago, He had chosen to come to me in the form of a baby boy, to hold me, to rescue me, and to redeem my life. I believe that was the only day Otis ever tried to hug me while getting his diaper changed.

That day opened my eyes to how God wanted me to embrace my identity as a mom. He exposed the old TV spotlight as a false light compared to the light He wanted to develop in my life as a mother. He revealed to me His great love for moms and their holy task of raising up the children He has designed. I felt God showing and telling me the simple value of being a mom.

As that discovery unfolded, I realized that waking up from a nap with my child's arms wrapped around me; filling days with story-reading, stroller walks, homemade science experiments, and games of hide-n-seek; pitching endlessly to a young batter; and taking trips to the grocery store with a daughter dressed as a princess-of-the-week—those things were more important to me than rising early to an alarm, grabbing a Starbucks, and rushing off to another day in the TV limelight.

This isn't to suggest that I think staying home to snuggle and play with your kids is the only way to be a good mom. This is not a treatise on the superiority of stay-at-home motherhood. Whether you're a mom working at home or away from home, either way you can be a dedicated mom who understands that God created motherhood as a sacred post in the life of a woman.

Allow me to use an illustration to prove my point about your mom role being sacred. During my time in television, I won an Emmy award for my political reporting. Over the years, I have used this Emmy as a prop when giving speeches to various mom groups. I ask the moms in the audience to compare two events that I reenact in front of them.

First, I throw down "a red carpet" (a red towel) and ask the moms to clap for me as I walk down that red carpet with my Emmy award hoisted in the air. They kindly give me a round of gracious applause. Then I put my Emmy away and kneel down on the red carpet (which, conveniently, has become a towel again). I invite one mom from the audience to sit in a chair next to the towel. I then place this mom's feet into a tub of warm water and I gently wash them, toes, heels and all.

After I complete these two exercises (and give the mom the red towel for her feet), I ask the women in the audience a few questions. I inquire, "which of those two events, walking the red carpet or washing the feet, would the world say is more important? They answer, "walking the red carpet." Then I ask, which one of these tasks is a mom more likely to do? The know this. They say, "wash feet." And finally, I ask, which one of these tasks did Jesus ask us to do? The answer is obvious. And this is just one more proof that a mom's work, even when it seems mundane, is sacred.

****

It was like I'd suddenly woken up to the incredible meaning behind family and mothering. When that idea took hold, I made it my urgent mission to spread this message to moms everywhere. I pondered, I prayed, and I produced proposals on what form this new mission should take.

One night I woke up and felt like God gave me the word "ChannelMom." It was a word that carried a double meaning. First, it would be a literal media channel for moms (on TV, radio and YouTube) and, second, it would be a "channel of living water," so to speak, offering moms hope, encouragement and advice. We'd broadcast the importance of motherhood by creating our own channels to do it.

ChannelMom Media developed very slowly, from a website, into a Denver radio show, into a syndicated radio show and now, broadcasting media on various platforms. Today, moms can access our programming all over the world. We became a nonprofit in 2014, still with the goal of ministering to moms through the airwaves, but also providing outreach on the ground. ChannelMom Outreach now provides several services for marginalized moms:

1) Homeless Outreach, assigning mentors to help single moms (and their kids) transition out of homelessness; 2) Prison Outreach, offering incarcerated moms instruction on inner healing and healthy parenting to stop the cycle of incarceration that typically gets passed down from parent to child; and 3) Single Mom Outreach, supporting single moms through bill payments, household goods, and gifts beginning in the Christmas season, but often extending throughout the year.

****

If you've ever had a dream or goal that seemed like it was never going to happen, I've got something to confess. As I was striving to build ChannelMom into something, it felt like God kept tapping the brakes. I've since realized His divine mercy was in that hold-your-horses process. ChannelMom grew slowly enough that I had enough time to commit to being a dedicated mom. Ironic, right? I'm Type-A-ambitious and I had planned to build ChannelMom quickly and big. But that would have drawn me away from the important task of being a mom—the very purpose I was promoting! Maybe this gives you hope for the pauses in your life or the years of being "on hold." Trust the good reasons behind the slow unfolding.

I had the luxury of being able to stay at home and mother my children for many years (partly because my husband was willing to be the sole breadwinner), as I slowly built ChannelMom on the side. I was able to dive into a firsthand education on being a mom, first for my children and second for the thousands of moms I aimed to encourage.

In those precious mothering years, my family was blessed with lots of joy and laughter, but we also faced some trials. I believe our trials teach us. And we have the opportunity to pass on the lessons we've learned to our children. As trials touched our family, I aimed to capture those teachable moments for our kids.

I believe our trials teach us.

We've been through a school shooting, the loss of close friends, our children's back-to-back surgeries and, finally, a breast cancer diagnosis. There were big lessons in each of these that affected and informed my mothering. I think it's so important to turn our problems into "teachers" for ourselves and our kids. If you instruct your children now to see their trials as teachable moments, it could become a lifelong habit that serves them well.

****

In 2006, my husband Mike was the assistant principal at Platte Canyon High School in Bailey, Colorado. On September 27th of that year, a 53-year-old gunman walked into the school and into a classroom, where he took multiple hostages.

My best friend (a mom) happened to be visiting the school when the gunmen made his entrance. She called me while hiding beneath a desk, whispering over the phone that there was "a shooter in the school." I didn't believe her. She quietly insisted that she wasn't kidding. She tried to reassure me that my husband was alright, but I later found out that he'd been in jeopardy. A sheriff's deputy who was clearing the halls did not recognize my husband as he approached from the other end of a hallway, so the deputy did his job and drew on my husband. Fortunately, in our small town, all my husband had to say, with his hands in the air, was "It's Schmitty, it's Schmitty." The deputy recognized the name and lowered his gun.

My frightened friend had taken the risk of phoning me as the school went into lockdown (the gunman wasn't in her immediate vicinity) simply to ask me to pray. To get everyone to pray. I hung up and called people to ask them for prayer. We set up a prayer chain of sorts and prayed for the high school, the students, the teachers and the staff. We prayed for the whole school district. Our son was in the elementary school down the road from the high school. His school was also in lockdown. In all honesty, there were a few moments when I did not know if either my husband or my son was safe.

The high school actually had significant security measures in place, but the ex-military killer found a way to skirt the security. In an hours-long ordeal, the gunman narrowed his group of hostages down to six female students. It's not worth sharing the abuse he imposed on those girls.

In the end, he kept only one hostage, a girl named Emily Keyes. As the SWAT team broke into the room where Emily was being held, the gunman simultaneously aimed his gun at this 16-year-old girl and shot her in the back. Emily died within minutes, not long after sending her family the now famous text, "I love u guys." Emily left behind her twin brother Casey and her parents John-Michael and Ellen, who were forced to face life without their beloved sister and daughter.

My husband was devastated that the school had lost one of their own. In the months preceding the tragedy, he had some eerie premonitions about the high school being in jeopardy. He and other staff had put into place a number of new security measures. Mike had also proposed additional steps to beef up security, but these were turned down by an advisory group that thought it highly unlikely that a school shooting would ever infiltrate our tiny, rural town. But it did, unfolding on the very day our son was turning eight. We had planned a special evening birthday celebration, but Mike had to stay at the school for debriefing with law enforcement. Our little boy didn't understand why his dad couldn't come home for his birthday.

In the days that followed the shooting, our young children watched the aftermath. Otis was upset that it had occurred on his birthday, explaining that he wasn't sure he could ever enjoy his birthday again. Our daughter Georgia was only four, but she was deeply aware that our community had suffered a great loss.

We cried in front of our kids. We reminisced about Emily's life (my husband had actually gotten to know her one semester when he tutored her in math). We prayed for Emily's family. We mourned with and supported our grieving community. Our children watched this process of dealing with devastating loss. They saw what adults do to help themselves and to support others. They learned about community. They learned about entering into grief on behalf of others. The lessons learned during that difficult time would serve our children well in the years to come. Any tough lessons that unfold in your family's future hold the potential to serve your kids well too. It makes the hard times easier if you can remember that.

****

Fast forward several years to 2010, when our family embarked upon a grueling season of loss. My other very best friend lost her husband in a motorcycle wreck. Honestly, he seemed too strong to die. He'd been a Navy Seal and a military contractor—strong, brave, true to his family and friends. He was only 36. He left behind my precious friend, only 33, and their two children, ages 12 and 10. This was a season of mourning and giving for our family.

I remember our son staying very close to my friend's 10-year-old son that first night after his dad had died. Otis insisted on watching over this boy as he slept through the night, so that he wouldn't feel alone. In the days that followed, we would sleep in that house often. My kids would play with their daughter and son daily. We'd help with funeral plans and meals, outings and vacations. We made a point of being at their home nearly every day for over a year. My kids learned how to go through grief with those who are suffering and to give generously again and again. None of us was perfect in our service to this family, but my kids learned important lessons.

In the next few years, we would lose almost a dozen friends and family members. Some died in car accidents. Some succumbed to cancer. And two of my son's teenaged friends committed suicide. Again and again, our kids were called upon to step up and minister. I remember one day when my daughter asked, "When is it going to stop, Mommy, all this death?" Partly to reassure myself, I kept telling my kids that God was teaching them and counting on them to help the hurting. He was trusting them to show compassion and grace to those in need. I guess these are things they needed to learn before they would each face trials of their own.

****

Growing up in a small town, our son Otis had always been labeled a "gifted student" and was able to stand out as an athlete as well. But when he tore the labrum in his shoulder during a baseball game, he was eventually forced to the sidelines. I should mention that he first finished the baseball season (pitching with a torn labrum, believe it or not) and he insisted on playing through the football season too—despite his injury.

Following a successful surgery in the winter, his recovery forced him to sit out most of basketball season and an entire season of baseball. Then, a year later, he tore his ACL—in his final basketball game as a high school senior. He was devastated to be sidelined once again. And I was a bit devastated that he would have to go through yet another surgery and I would have to trudge through more worry.

Now is the time to admit that I have been a lifelong worrier. I have succumbed to fear far too easily. Each time Otis faced a surgery, I would worry that something would go terribly wrong. He tried not to show any signs of worry himself, but I know he felt trepidation too.

Beyond his trepidation lay more teachable moments. My son was forced to face the vulnerability of his body and the temporal nature of his athletic career. These were lessons in humility. My son realized what it was like to be the guy on the bench, missing the cheers and accolades. He saw what it felt like to have a body that didn't work the way he wanted. He also realized the degree to which he had derived his self-worth from his athletic and academic achievements. And this mom realized how much pride she'd taken in those same things.

As the mom, I had to take a step back and recognize the way in which I'd leaned into my kids' accomplishments, sometimes to the detriment of developing their character. Because I was so proud of how well they did in academics and athletics, I sometimes overlooked their need for humility and for grace toward those who didn't share the same gifts but had unique gifts of their own.

I'm not suggesting that we should not cheer on our children and be pleased with their achievements; however, we must not let character be sacrificed in the process. In the last few years, I've tried harder to look beyond academic awards and athletic feats in order to instruct our children to see the unique gifts in others, to be quick to forgive, to offer grace, and to understand the value of making peace. I've also tried to direct their focus toward the virtues of humility and sacrifice.

They're still learning and I'm still teaching (and learning). Again, we're not perfect at these things. Still, I was pleased a few years back when my son called from college with a reminder that his character was, indeed, being shaped. He was discouraged about being unable to play football in his freshman year (he was still recovering from ACL surgery). Instead, he was assigned to videotape practices, sometimes in the rain, and also to run cameras from behind the bleachers during games. He felt lost and rejected. As he described these feelings to me, he said, rather haltingly, and perhaps fighting the urge to cry, "I think God is trying to teach me humility, Mom." Maybe He is, son, maybe He is.

****

The year 2018 began with sickness and injury. In January, I went through one of the worst bouts of flu I'd ever experienced and our daughter Georgia broke her arm in her very first "club" volleyball tournament. She was shattered by the fact that she would not be able to play volleyball for the rest of the club season.

The injury was significant, with complete breaks of the major bones in her forearm. When I learned how serious the breaks were (during our trip to the ER), it made me all the more impressed that Georgia had gone back into the volleyball game to try to continue playing. She was tough through the whole ordeal, refusing to cry, even when it took more than two hours to get painkillers.

Surgery was scheduled and Georgia was looking forward to getting "fixed." I, on the other hand, was nervous. I quickly sank into my debilitating habit of fear and worst-case-scenario thinking. Georgia had the opposite reaction. She schooled me in the practice of peace and faith. She was joking with the nurses before going into surgery and didn't have any visible signs of concern. She made it through the surgery beautifully. I thanked God profusely and we settled in for the recovery process.

As Georgia was recovering, I began watching my 50-something body go through a series of breakdowns, from venous disease, to chronic headaches, to vision problems, to weakness in my arms and legs. Then, in the summer, I poked myself in the eye and developed a giant blood blister.

Just as I seemed to be running out of ailments, I went in for a mammogram. It had been several years since I'd had one. The process seemed fairly routine until the technicians asked me to stay. After a nervous and lonely time in the waiting room, I was called in to speak to the radiologist. He explained that he believed I had a small cancerous lump in my left breast. I was strangely calm, but I also felt sick and scared. I remember getting details from the office staff about how I should proceed—appointments I needed to make, insurance I needed to arrange.

I have a vivid memory of what it felt like to walk back to my car and get in, asking God why He could be allowing such a thing. I was confused and frightened. Fear would haunt me in the days that followed. I informed my husband, not knowing yet how small or large the cancer was. My worst moments came from fear and not from facts. I remember lying in bed the night of the diagnosis and feeling almost catatonic, as if I couldn't move or smile or believe or hope. My mind went dark, fixated on worst-case scenarios and thoughts of leaving my kids behind if I were to die in the coming year.

Our 30th wedding anniversary celebration was ahead of us, and we had big plans to go on a Caribbean cruise as a family. I enjoy being a fun and active mom, so I was devastated by the thought of potentially being sickly on the cruise ship.

This is the thing about fear. It doesn't tell us the truth. It robs us of hope. But God showed me that fear was wrong and faith came through—in the form of a nurse and a radiologist.

> *This is the thing about fear. It doesn't tell us the truth.*

During the biopsy, while lying on the table, I began to cry. And those two amazing women gently began to rescue me from my fears. The radiologist called the tumor "itty-bitty." And the nurse, who had lost her mom to breast cancer many years earlier, told me how fortunate I was to be living in the 21st century, when breast cancer treatment is so effective. They both assured me that I was probably going to live.

Later I learned that the cancer was slow-growing, had been caught early (stage 1) and was not the type that needed chemotherapy. When the lab nurse delivered this good news to me over the phone, I cried happy tears. I think I almost made her cry too. I thanked her profusely and hung up. I then fell to the floor, sobbing (loud sobbing) more tears of joy and relief and thanking God for His grace.

The next happy-tears moment came when my husband and I met with my surgeon, Dr. Jane Kercher, a spunky, effervescent woman of faith. One of the first things she announced to me and my husband was, "Well, you're not going to die from this." Tears again. We were both immensely grateful and relieved.

I must say that I know not everyone receives good news like this. There were days when I almost felt guilty for such a positive prognosis. I hesitated to share it with many people—partly because I didn't want to tell people I had any kind of cancer and partly because I knew there were people who had suffered through much worse. I was also haunted by the story of Kara Tippetts (featured in Chapter 8). She had been diagnosed with stage 4 breast cancer and died at age 38, leaving her four young children behind. I worried that, if it happened to Kara, it could happen to me. So, despite the reassuring prognosis, irrational fears continued to haunt me.

Before my lumpectomy surgery, I was feeling quite afraid; however, on the day of surgery, I learned an inescapable lesson. Surrender. As I lay there in my surgical cap and gown, waiting to be rolled into the operating room, I had a moment of panic. I suddenly thought, I don't want to do this. What if I die on the operating table? What if it doesn't go well? And then I realized that, despite my objections, I was in the hands of God and the hands of some well-trained nurses and doctors. I had to trust. I had no other choice.

Surgery went well, and radiation was easier than I thought it would be. I was declared cancer-free. And I was a healthy, happy woman on our anniversary cruise.

I am newly grateful for the capable women and men in our medical community. I had been somewhat skeptical of traditional medicine, but seeing the effective outcome of my medical treatment helped change my mind. But it didn't cure my nagging fears, which continued to plague me for almost a year after my successful surgery. I fixated on death and the fact that we all must face it someday. I worried about another cancer diagnosis. I worried about worrying. And I feared being fearful.

And you know what? I've had it. I'm over it.

As a woman who loves the Lord, I've requested that He be the professor of my "Overcoming Fear 101" class. I've asked God to make me a woman of faith and not of fear—to bring me to a place of trusting Him fully for this life and the next.

You know why? Because I want to pass on a legacy of faith to our children, not a legacy of fear. I want them to believe that God is good, that He loves them and that He is faithful. He has proven faithful again and again in our lives. I am finally walking the long, slow road to completely trusting His faithfulness.

I have heard the Holy Spirit whisper words of reassurance and hope to me. I've heard Him assure me that I am well and that He loves me. I have leaned into scriptures like, "My grace is sufficient for you"; "I am the Lord, who heals you"; and "In all things God works for the good of those who love Him, who have been called according to His purpose." Before Jesus left the earth, He assured us that worry was a waste of time and fear was foolish: "Do not worry about your life"; "Do not worry about tomorrow"; "Do not be afraid"; and "Be of good cheer, I have overcome the world."

I keep my heart focused on my personal belief that Jesus died for death, for sin, for hate, for hurt and for fear. That He paid for every bad thing in this world, where each of us is free to choose to do bad things. That He has a place for us in Heaven, where life is better and lasts forever. These are the things I hold onto, as I crawl, millimeter by millimeter, away from fear. Faith feels good. It's the better way. And I want to pass it on to my children and to the many moms I minister to. Help me, God!

Not only do I seek God's help, I thank Him. I'm thankful that He allowed my TV job to be taken away in the midst of turning me into a mom. I'm thankful that He ended up showing me the better thing. In fact, I believe motherhood is often the vehicle God uses to introduce Himself to His creation... caring, nurturing, instructing, loving, redeeming and rescuing through the hands of a mother.

I can even thank God for allowing me to go through the experience of cancer. It was humbling. Even though I'd been a lifelong exerciser, had lots of energy and thought of myself as a strong woman who helped other people, I came to the end of myself. I needed help from God and people. I had weaknesses, just like everyone else. The cancer equipped me to encourage other moms who have been humbled by their circumstances. Moms in prison. Moms who are homeless. Moms who are struggling. Please remember that your pain and even your children's pain can have a purpose. To identify with others' pain and to help them through it.

****

So, there it is. I've shared some of the biggest secrets behind my own mothering. It makes me think of the saying that goes, "the hand that rocks the cradle rules the world." I happen to believe most moms want to "rule" well by being the very best moms they can be.

My own mothering secrets and the other moms' secrets that follow—discovered in the midst of fame, fortune, disease and despair—can help you be the amazing mom you want to be for your own precious kids.

My Amazing Mom Secret:

Believe that being a mom is incredibly important.

Why You Are Amazing #1
(re-read often)

You, mom, are the person who keeps life going. You literally keep things alive. Kids. Pets. Plants. You feed. You nurture. You heal. YOU are responsible for raising up the next generation. This world depends on your dedication as a mom... even if it doesn't tell you.

Chapter 2
The Power of Forgiveness
Yvonne Pointer

If your daughter was brutally murdered as she trudged through the snow on her way to school, would you forgive the killer? Would you make plans to visit him in prison? Yvonne Pointer's answers to these tough questions might shock you, but they also might change your life.

❀❀❀❀❀❀

I'll admit it. The story of Gloria and Yvonne Pointer wrecks me. It wrecks me because it involves the one thing every mom dreads: the death of a child.

14-year-old Gloria Pointer was raped and murdered on December 6, 1984. It happened while she was on her way to school. Her body was later found in the snow outside an abandoned building.

Her mom's response to this horrific event was to do what she'd always done—devote herself to acting on behalf of her daughter, even in death.

> Her body was so severely beaten it took three to four days before I got a chance to see her. When I saw her for the first time, she was in the casket at the funeral home. I told everybody that wanted to go with me, I said, 'No, I need to do this myself.' So, I went by myself and I pulled a chair up to the casket, and I just sat there and I looked, and I said, 'How did this happen? How did this happen? How did you end up in this casket?'
>
> And I said, 'I promise you that I will find out who did this.' I said, 'After all the work and the effort, the sacrifices—they're not gonna just take your life and I don't do anything about it. That's not going to happen. The person will say that he is sorry.' That's what I said. Now I just didn't know at the time that it was gonna take twenty-nine years."

Over her daughter's casket, in the suffocating silence, Yvonne made a vow to her Gloria: "I said, 'I'm gonna find out what happened and your death will not be in vain.'" This vow launched a mother's search for her daughter's killer that would drag on for decades.

The story of Yvonne and Gloria Pointer is a mother-daughter chronicle that is both tragic and inspirational. It's a story that begins and ends in Cleveland, Ohio. Yvonne was the fourth-born of ten children. Her family struggled to make ends meet. She recalls that her mother always seemed to be working to contribute to the family income. As a result, her mom had very little time to focus on her kids. It was in the midst of this austere family environment that Yvonne became pregnant. She was just sixteen years old.

"The strangest thing is, I didn't even know I was pregnant. It was my mother that really knew before I did. Because, with the girls, she had a way of monitoring the number of sanitary napkins we were using, and she noticed that I was not coming in to get them. So, she made an appointment for me to go to the hospital and be checked. And indeed, I was pregnant. So that is how I found out."

Knowing the shock that can accompany teen pregnancy, I asked how she responded to her looming motherhood. "I didn't have a thought," she says. "I was too young to know anything. I was a straight A student who now had to drop out of school, because at that time you could not go to school pregnant. So, I wasn't like all excited. I was just, like, I don't know what to do. Life was changed."

That change—from straight A student to pregnant teen dropout—caused Yvonne to vow that her baby daughter Gloria would have a life different from her own. "I knew that I wanted her life to be different. The thing that derailed my education, my hope for my future, I wanted it to be different for her. So, I was gonna do everything differently. My mother didn't have time for individuals, so I was going to be focused, laser focused, on guiding [Gloria] through the landmines of life."

Yvonne focused on two landmines that had derailed her own youthful plans. "That she stayed in school and didn't get pregnant. I think that was it—that school was her priority and not boys. As she grew older and she wanted to go over to someone's house, I would limit the time that she could be out of my sight. I would always say, if she did get into something, she wouldn't have a lot of time to do it, cuz she had to be back by a certain time."

As she swept away the landmines, Yvonne had another focus. She made a commitment to being present for Gloria. "I wanted her to have the presence of her mother."

Yvonne recalls the deep hurt of missing her own mother's presence, "Back in those days, they had open house [at school], and my mother never could come because she worked. I mean, I was very judgmental against her, if I might say. And I would see all the other mothers there, and I could never understand, at that time, where was my mother? I have to be honest. I was critical. Like she doesn't care enough to come."

As Yvonne wrestled with negative judgements of her mom, something positive broke through: those tough judgments became Yvonne's motivation to do more and be more for her own daughter. "I went to everything she did at her school. As a single mother, it was very financially difficult, so I couldn't afford to do the things that the other kids' mothers did, but she had something the other kids didn't have and that was her mother. Present." She carried this "present mom" philosophy into parenting her two younger children as well.

Yvonne applied her vision of being present for her kids, despite the fact that it was never modeled during her own childhood. But she admits that her ambitious vision was not always reflected in her everyday mothering.

"As single mothers, keep in mind that it's not always possible. You have to work. So, I had to work, but then I always made sure that whatever [Gloria] was involved with, that I celebrated. I was present. Sometimes, [in other] families, the children, they have all the stuff. The parents work so the children will have the stuff. She didn't have the stuff. She had me." However, Yvonne once moved heaven and earth to come up with particular "stuff" her daughter needed.

> I never will forget. She had something that she needed—a pair of tennis shoes—and I had no money. None. So, I went to the Goodwill and I found these tennis shoes for like a quarter, I think. I think they were brand new. And I made it to the school in time. As I was down on the floor tying them up, she hugged my neck until we lost our balance and we both fell over. She was just so appreciative. That's why she would always say, "My mother will do it." That was her favorite line. I don't care if it was somebody else going through something in her school, she would always say, "Don't worry, my mother will do it."

"My mother will do it" is a phrase Yvonne clings to. Maybe it serves as a reminder of her daughter's faith in her—in her ability to do what Gloria (or anyone else) needed to have done. Maybe the sound of those five words is a visceral connection to Gloria's daughterly affection. Maybe this helps Yvonne bridge the chasm of death that now separates their mother-daughter love.

Yvonne recalls how she lived out that "my mother will do it" mantra while her kids were growing up. She recollects how she helped one neighborhood boy who was in need of some motherly love:

> Years ago, he would be bullied. They didn't call it bullied then. They'd just mess with him. I would go to the library and get books and then come and sit on the porch and read to him. He would come and knock on the door and say to my kids, "Can your mother come out and play?" My daughter Danielle would say, "Get away from my door. My mother ain't no child." I'd say "Leave him alone!" And I would go out and say, "Do you have a book again today?" What was he looking for? That mother. Somebody that says I care about you.

Yvonne's care spilled out for the neighborhood children, just as it did for her own. Even the smallest things. "We didn't have money. If the kids wanted popsicles, we didn't have the money. Everybody could get popsicles from the truck. What I would do is, I would get things for them to sell to the kids with the money, and they could buy the popsicles when the truck came."

Do you see what I see? Yvonne was a mom who would find a way. A mom who was there for her kids. Involved. Committed. Protective. Reliable. She was the "my mother will do it" mom. This is the thing that makes Gloria's untimely death even more difficult to comprehend. How could Yvonne Pointer's daughter be vulnerable to a criminal's attack? Not Yvonne's daughter. Yvonne watched over Gloria like a hawk:

I think that is a part of the grief process that I went through. What more could I have done... you did everything, you were there, but you still had that grief. Oh, what could I have done? We didn't even have an income.

We delivered newspapers from *The Plain Dealer*. My son and I would go out and deliver the papers, and she [Gloria] would get my other daughter on the school bus and they'd go to school. She would meet up with her friends. And even that was calculated. "Don't go through the alleys," I would say to her. "Stay on the main street. Just be careful."

And even that morning, when I was delivering the newspapers, we saw her walking to school and I let down the window. I said, "Why are you going through this alley. Didn't I tell you not to go through the alley?" And it seems as if my voice was caught by the wind and went up. It felt like it was a megaphone on my voice. And I was thinking, "Why are you screaming at her?" And I said, "I told you, don't go through this alley, so get to school and hurry up."

I pulled away just a few minutes and I thought to myself, maybe I should give her a ride. And I looked in the car, which was piled high with newspapers. There was nowhere for her to sit. And I thought, oh, she'll be okay, but I'm gonna give it to her later. That's the day she died. So, when people say, "Well, why didn't that mother get up and take her to school?" they don't realize that I was already out

trying to make a living for us by delivering
newspapers.

As Yvonne re-lived that horrible day, I thought about my
own daughter who had just celebrated her fifteenth
birthday. Gloria had been just one year younger when she
was murdered. Realizing the priceless presence of my own
teenage girl made the horror of Gloria's death personal for
me.

I told Yvonne that I simply could not fathom such a loss.
"Well, you have a lot of denial," Yvonne responded. "You
do. You don't realize it, because I still had expectations that
it was some horrible nightmare and that she would be
coming home—even up to and after the funeral. I mean,
even now, you still expect them to come. When I'm working
with families, people say, 'Oh, you'll get over it.' No, you do
not. No, you do not. Your life—this is my favorite line—as
you know it, the normal life that you had is no longer
normal. So now you have to find a new normal. A new
reason to live. A new reason—to exist."

A reason for a mom to continue to exist? After the brutal
death of her sweet, firstborn daughter. Her bright and
constant star. Her straight A student with perfect
attendance. The daughter stolen from her—wrenched away
on a dark, wintry day.

I have imagined that Yvonne's soul must have reflected
the wintry crime scene where her daughter died. Cold.
Bitter. Abandoned. And alone. A mother's soul, bereft. No
longer able to soak in the presence of her Gloria.

Without Gloria's presence, Yvonne was left to love her
deceased daughter however she could. She became
determined to uncover what had happened to her girl, to
find Gloria's killer herself: "I mean, I looked for him. That's

how I ended up going into the prisons. I still do that after thirty-something years. Everywhere I thought he would be, under every rock, I turned it over and I went in. Through midnight basketball, working with people in the streets, working with the lowly, the drug addicts. I'm looking for this person."

But her dedication was tested. The search took years longer than Yvonne ever anticipated, "So [when] the DNA test revealed who he was after twenty-nine years, it wasn't like I was sitting twiddling my thumbs. I was cleaning out some papers the other day, and I was looking at all the letters. I was writing letters to presidents. I was writing letters to anybody, to Oprah—that's how I ended up on the Oprah Winfrey Show. I just wanted somebody to help me find this person, even the Attorney General's office. Anybody."

Yvonne says she'd always had a love for books and the written word, so this gave her the stamina to write...and write...and write, in her quest to find Gloria's killer. "I was always writing letters, trying to get someone greater than myself to come to help me, only to find out that I was the person that I was looking for." Just like Gloria used to say, "My mother will do it," after all the writing and all the pleas, Yvonne finally realized she would have to be the one to do it.

"I became the person. People see me today, but you don't know that I was longing for insanity, begging God to let me die. I did not want to live with that kind of pain. So, when the DNA test came back and they found the man, I can say to you honestly that I had already forgiven the person."

The person receiving Yvonne's unfathomable forgiveness was a man named Hernandez Warren. He was the one who ambushed Gloria on her way to school—a day she was extra eager to attend. You see, Gloria was scheduled to receive an award for perfect attendance on that very day—the day she was raped and killed. It's agonizing to reflect on this sweet daughter's joyful anticipation, brutally cut short in the cold of a winter day.

Yet, somehow, this mother forgives. She forgives the unthinkable act.

Yet, somehow, this mother forgives. She forgives the unthinkable act. She forgives her very own daughter's killer. She forgives, even though she waited nearly three decades to hear this man utter the words, "I'm sorry," in a courtroom.

In a news report about Gloria's murder, published in the *Cleveland Plain Dealer*, Warren is quoted as saying, "I deserve to die." The article explained further:

> In a videotaped interview... in Cuyahoga County Common Pleas Court, Hernandez Warren told officers that he was high on drugs when he lured Gloria to a back stairwell of a building on East 105th Street as she walked to school. He said he raped her in the stairwell and then began to leave. As he did, Gloria attempted to leave. That's when he pushed her down the stairs and beat her with a brick or pipe that had been nearby, according to his statement. He said the last thing the girl did was call for her mother, according to the videotape.

> And, since that last day her daughter called her name, Gloria's mother has answered. Not only did she search for her daughter's killer for twenty-nine

years in her visits to troubled tribes—men in prisons and boys in youth basketball clubs—she has generously parlayed her efforts into a mission of comfort and hope for vulnerable young people—youngsters in schools and orphans in Africa.

Yvonne had searched for Hernandez Warren for decades. Once he was found, she began to visit this man—her daughter's killer— in prison. Repeatedly. She made it her mission to make Warren understand that Gloria's death was not in vain. "'Gloria Pointer is more than just a murdered child,' I told him. When I went to visit him in the prison, I said, 'You may not know that she lives on through so many things.' He cried. Oh my God, he cried.

I didn't want to talk to him about Gloria. I wanted him to help me—help me to understand the mindset, so that we could save the children. Cuz, what do we look for? What did I miss? What are we still missing? He couldn't help me, because he was crying so hard."

Even during his trial, Warren had not been able to answer questions like Yvonne's. "I killed her, but why and how, I don't know," Warren told Cleveland police officers, as reported by *The Plain Dealer*. "I was [messed] up. I was [messed] up."

Hiding behind Warren's tears was a background you might not expect from a man convicted of raping and murdering a child. Personally, I'd conjured up an image of him having a terrible childhood of abuse that had predictably shaped him into a violent criminal.

But Yvonne countered my stereotyped image with an alternate story of Warren's life: "He had a privileged childhood. His family was always getting him out of trouble. As a matter of fact, some years after the case was filed, somebody who grew up in their community said he always felt that they should have investigated him [Hernandez], because [he] had raped his little sister. Everybody knew he was a rapist. Everybody knew it. And his family would just always give money to people, so they wouldn't prosecute him and stuff like that."

I wonder how a different parental approach toward a young Hernandez Warren would have changed things. What if his parents hadn't repeatedly bailed him out? What if they'd actually made him pay the price? Would he have raped and murdered Gloria all those years later?

****

Yvonne would be the first to tell you about the enormity of parental influence. She can tell you how it impacted the hearts and minds of criminals she met during her prison visits. It came in a variety of forms. A lack of parental presence...a scarcity of fatherly instruction...or a missing motherly love. Yvonne saw each of these missing parenting pieces in the haphazard puzzles of prisoners' dysfunctional lives. After all, she had a ringside seat for many inmate stories during her three-decades-long search for Hernandez Warren:

> When I would go into the prison, I would say, "If you're in this crowd," cuz I'm addressing hundreds of men, "I want you to know that I forgive you. I just need to hear you say, 'I'm sorry.'" I had prisoners who had done worse things than that. They would love on me and they would apologize for him and [say] "We're so sorry."

So, now, because I was receiving sympathy from these murderers and rapists and pedophiles, I'd say, "Well, what is your story? Why are you here?" And then I got to hear their stories. Oh my God, everybody has a story. I heard about their molestation as a child and their anger at their mothers. I heard about all of this. So that made me want to show them love, because they were showing me so much love, so much so [that] I'll tell you, when the arrest was made [of Hernandez Warren], I had to go to a local prison, because pandemonium broke out. The people from the prison called and said, "You gotta come here so they [the inmates] can see that you're okay."

Yvonne says prisoners continue to show concern for her to this day, years after Warren was convicted of Gloria's murder. "I was in the prison last week, and all they said was, 'Are you okay? Are you okay?' As a matter of fact, do you know they send me money to help me with the kids in Africa? They have bought bikes. I'm talking about inmates. They buy food. They want to make clothing, 'cuz this gives them hope for their life." Yvonne works to give them hope, displaying remarkable sympathy for these hardened prisoners. Including the one who victimized her own family.

If you've ever been the victim of a crime, you may have zero sympathy for men like these. Not Yvonne. Her heart has been softened by their stories—stories of alarming hurt hiding behind their heinous acts:

One young man in prison—he's a violent offender. He didn't just take your purse when he robbed you, he beat you mercilessly. So, one day, after ten years of going to this prison, he scooted over next to me and he said, "I'm going to tell you something that I've only told one other person in life." At that time Gloria's case wasn't solved, so I really expected him to say, "I murdered your daughter." That's where my mind was, because that's why I'm in the prison, looking for a killer.

He goes on to tell me about his horrific childhood. His mother was on drugs. His mother was dating the drug dealer who used to give him weed at the age of ten. He was thinking he was having all this fun. His mother has got this drug-dealing boyfriend, they've got all this money. Well, one night the drug-dealer boyfriend comes out of the bathroom dressed like a woman and proceeds to molest him. And this went on for years.

Yvonne offers graphic details (too graphic to share) of unimaginable abuse perpetrated upon this young boy, including being threatened with a gun while he was being molested. Yvonne believes it was that violent abuse that turned the boy into a man of violence. "He explained that he did what he did because he was mad at his mother. Every time he robbed a woman, he

From this day forward, you have a mother.

did it to get back at his mother. So, the poor innocent victim, she had no idea that it's because he felt unprotected by his mother that that person was suffering the consequences."

In response to sickening stories like these, Yvonne began to offer herself up as the loving mom these prisoners never had:

> I went to a prison once, and I always talk about Gloria, so the inmates know about it. And one guy said, "I have a question to ask you. How is it possible for you to still love a child who is not alive and my mother, who is alive, has no love for me?" When he said it, I got up from behind the podium and went to the aisle, and I opened my arms. I said, "Come here," and I wrapped my arms around him. I said, "From this day forward, you have a mother." And he collapsed and sobbed. He sobbed. He sobbed. So, you can't even imagine... to not have your mother. I know a lot of people say "My father was never there," but the mother is supposed to love you and nurture you. I just think it's essential to the development of society, especially a violence-plagued society.

I have to admit something. I feel self-conscious when I think about the horrific stories that Yvonne Pointer willingly enters into. I feel like a privileged, middle-class white woman who simply cannot know what is known by Yvonne—this self-appointed mother to so many damaged people:

> Mayor Michael R. White called me the mother of Cleveland, because I'm the mother, supposedly, to so many. As a matter of fact, I'm at schools now. This generation, it's just... I don't want to use the word "lost" lightly, but I will use the word "lost," because this is the second generation of drug-addicted children. They come up without any guidance. I go

into these schools all the time, just trying to drop a little love in. And [in] the schools, mostly, are the girls who've been kicked out of regular school—the troubled girls, so I know there's power in a mother's love and in a mother's touch, just like the absence of that is detrimental.

Yvonne Pointer represents the power of "mother." She's filled the void of her own "mom loss," by mothering many others. Her mothering aims to reach far and wide through an impressive array of endeavors. Yvonne has established a midnight basketball league in Cleveland for underprivileged youth. She mentors kids in inner-city schools. She visits men in prison. She's founded support groups for grieving parents. And she has raised funds to build schools for children in Ghana, West Africa.

It seems like there's a proverbial wind beneath Yvonne's wings that enables her to mother so many. Yvonne says she imagines Gloria on a heavenly perch, "sitting up and telling God, 'My mother will do it.'" Yvonne sees proof of this in what appear to be divine interventions, providing "a way" for her to do good in Gloria's memory. Recalling one such intervention, she wonders, "How do you explain somebody in Africa finding a piece of paper about Gloria's homicide, and now thousands of children are being fed and educated by somebody on the other side of the world?"

Here's how that unlikely intervention unfolded—in a way that miraculously connected Yvonne's good deeds to the other side of the world. In 2002, a teenager named Anthony Tay was walking down a street in Ghana, West Africa, distraught over struggles in his life and wondering if God really loved him. He'd been forced to drop out of school to help his mother make ends meet; many days he'd gone without food and wondered where his family's next meal would come from. As Anthony walked along, he saw a ripped piece of newspaper on the ground and picked it up. Unbelievably, the newspaper article was a story from the other side of the world about Yvonne Pointer and the struggles she faced in dealing with her daughter's murder. Anthony was moved to write a letter to Yvonne, expressing his sorrow over the murder of Gloria. He also told her about his dream of becoming a doctor and his hope of finding enough financial support to pursue his medical education. Upon reading the letter, Yvonne felt she was the one to provide that support and began sending money to Ghana to contribute to Anthony's education. Anthony Tay (then seventeen years old) was so moved by Yvonne's help, he vowed to help others in the way Yvonne had helped him, so he founded the Gloria Pointer Teen Movement Initiative in West Africa. Literature describing the Initiative explains that Anthony is now "dedicating his life to assist African youth in obtaining an education and healthy lifestyle in memory of Gloria."

It's like Yvonne's good deeds have been molded on the scriptural "potter's wheel," transforming the cold clay of unimaginable loss into the finished work of forgiveness and love. She admits she leaned into the biblical story of Joseph when she addressed Gloria's killer in court and told him she had already forgiven him. "[In] the speech that I gave to him, I used Joseph and all that [his] brothers had done to him. I walked him through it, so much until the judge cried. And I said, within that forty-ninth chapter, you will find that Joseph said to them [his brothers], 'You made it for evil, but God made it for good.'"

Yvonne clings to this idea of God making the evil of her daughter's murder into something "for good." Armed with that enduring hope, even as she walks with grief, Yvonne persists in doing good in Gloria's memory:

> Gloria used to always say to me, cuz I cried all the time, "Mom, I'm gonna make life better for you." She was going to marry a rich basketball player, and I was going to have this beautiful house. She would just always describe it. She said, "You're not going to have to cry forever."
>
> So that's kinda where it got started. And the strange thing about it, I have that life today. I have it. I travel the world. It's just absent of Gloria. So, I believe that she's just petitioned for me. I know that I have some kind of supernatural help in order to sustain and to do [what I do], to go to death row, and to pray for the person who murdered her. People always ask me, "How can you do this?" I just simply say, "I don't do it. I just avail myself to the Holy Spirit, so that He can do it through me."

As Yvonne gives credit to divine strength, her voice gives a hint of exhaustion, revealing her human limitations. She explains that, in just a few hours, she will be hosting a grieving family in her home. She tells me that the stream of grieving families never ends, frequently showing up on her doorstep or on the other end of her phone, always seeking her mothering comfort.

I ask if she's ever tempted to give up. "Every day," she admits, "because working with families over and over and over, you don't get to heal, because you're always pulling the scab off the wound."

"That's a sacrifice," I say, and she responds with a humble observation. "Well, it's a sacrifice that Jesus made, and if we say we're gonna be like Him, then we need to get ready to do some kind of sacrifice. Yours may not be like mine. When Martin Luther King [Jr.] was alive, I didn't understand why he didn't just stop. 'Dr. King, they're gonna kill you. Why don't you just stop?' But I get it today. He was sacrificing for the greater good."

I would like this greater good to extend to every single mom. I ask Yvonne what lessons she'd like to pass on to any mom reading this book. "Well, I would say, what would I give to have her walk in the door one more time, even if she was getting on my last nerve? Come on, mothers, I know they get on your nerves. I know they do. But can you imagine a life without them? That's the question. Just value the fact that you have them in your life."

Her reminder might hit a nerve for the mom who sometimes takes the presence of her children for granted. Yvonne punctuates her point by telling one last story of a child who could have used some good mothering. "We had a case here in Cleveland, where a little six-year-old boy was found wandering around the streets with only a t-shirt on, and you could see he had been duct-taped. They kept him in the basement and had him duct-taped to a bed. This is what his mother did to him. What kind of life scars is he gonna have from the person who's supposed to love him and nurture him?"

That question hits the mothering nail on the head. Yvonne has pointed to the great value and giant responsibility of a mom. It's a sacred responsibility. A mother's loving care gives life, while the lack of that care threatens life. And our culture forgets to place value on that life-giving role! Instead, we glorify the glamorous stuff, like big salaries, large homes, cool cars and sculpted bodies—all overshadowing the unglamorous roles like "mom."

A mother's loving care gives life, while the lack of that care threatens life.

Yvonne is eminently aware of the value of mothers—partly through the mothering she no longer gets to give her eldest child, partly through the mothering she sees missing in so many lives. But Yvonne is not one to condemn other mothers for where they may have failed.

Instead, she ends our conversation with a respectful challenge to every mom. Her challenge is this: "Mother more, mother well, mother those who need a mom, mother always, until you take your last breath."

Yvonne challenges us to be "step-in moms." She calls on all moms, not only to mother our own, but to serve as "step-in moms" whenever and wherever we're needed.

We end with Yvonne Pointer's mothering secret. When faced with the brutal loss of her daughter's precious life, Yvonne offered her own life as a lesson. A lesson of love witnessed by children in schools, men in prisons, staff in courtrooms, youngsters in Africa, officials in government, even her own family. Imagine the positive difference she has allowed her pain to make. A witness for forgiveness. An example for loving the unlovable.

Yvonne stands as a beacon of overcoming pain for the purpose of good. True and lasting good. She leaves all moms with a lesson she has personally lived. Turn your pain into purpose. Turn your pain into something good. Make a positive difference with the pain you've suffered and teach your kids to do the same.

Yvonne was heading off to do that very thing when she excused herself from our interview. A grieving family was headed to her home that evening to receive some of Yvonne's mother love. It's a love extended to families and children that are not hers... at least not until God puts them in her path. "I would say, we can ask God to give us strength to be mothers to more than the children we birthed. There's a whole lot of kids out there that need the mother's love. If not you, then who?"

Yvonne's Amazing Mom Secret:
Make a positive difference in response to your pain.

Why **You** Are Amazing #2
(re-read often)

You turn your pain into a positive for the sake of your kids. You transform your past pain—the stuff that really hurt you—and use it as a motivator to help others experiencing pain. You even choose to forgive those who caused your pain. Your children will take notice of what you do and, one day, they will do the same.

Chapter 3
Social Media Mayhem
Shelly Carlstrom

When instant fame led her only son down a path of social media hate and suicidal thoughts, this mom wasn't sure what to do. There was the week she hid him in her home. There were parental pep talks she never imagined giving to her grown child. And there were regrets. Regrets that she'd ever nominated her son to be on "The Bachelorette."

****

I'm not sure how to begin this mom's story. Mostly because there is so much. There are struggles. And scandals. And a sinful secret or two. Such salacious details threaten to overshadow the "amazing" behind this mom.

But if you were to get the inside view—the one her kids and friends have—then you'd be likely to spot the "amazing." Take the fact that, as a young mom, she purposely sought employment which allowed her to be near her kids every day—enabling her to be involved in their daily school activities and extracurricular events. She also overcame obstacles and mistakes, in a concerted effort to raise two children that folks would call "good kids." And she proved herself to be a steady champion for her son during one of the worst times of his life. As Shelly's daughter Tori explains, "my mom wakes up every day and she is a mom first." Tori says, even now, Shelly will drop everything to serve her and her brother whenever and wherever they need it.

Shelly's mothering story also happens to be relevant to our time. It's a modern mom drama with modern mothering issues. Most moms will identify with something in this story and every mom needs to hear it as a personal warning. A warning about twenty-first-century troubles your child is likely to face: social media "haters" who bully kids, "influencers" who take priority over parents, and reckless relationships that can develop online. These ominous adversaries come from a new world order that promotes unprecedented social and digital access and exposes our kids like never before.

Shelly's story is ensconced in this kind of exposure— exposure that resulted in overnight fame. Of course, most moms aren't famous and their kids aren't either. And, frankly, people shouldn't think that if someone lacks fame, it means they lack value. All moms and kids are valuable in countless ways, even though we fail to recognize that in our celebrity-obsessed culture. Shelly now sees the value of the "good ol' days" when fame wasn't part of her family's life.

****

Fame went viral in their lives when Shelly's son, Blake, was featured on the uber-popular television show, "*The Bachelorette.*" "*The Bachelorette*" is a part of the Bachelor/Bachelorette TV franchise that commands huge ratings. Specifically, "*The Bachelorette*" is a series on ABC that involves several dozen men vying for the hand of a featured bachelorette. The bachelorette gradually eliminates suitors over the eleven-week series until she chooses her man.

"*The Bachelorette*" catapulted Blake Horstmann to notoriety when he became the "runner-up" bachelor during the 2018 season. It's possible that Blake was the most popular runner-up ever... for a little while. Social media caught fire the night bachelorette Becca failed to choose Blake as her husband-to-be. She chose Garrett Yrigoyen instead and, as my son put it, "all of America was outraged." Twitter erupted the moment Blake was demoted to runner-up:

> "I love you, bye. BLAKE... IM CRYING I CAN'T HANDLE THIS #TheBacheloretteFinale #TheBachelorette"

> "The music is trying to trick us into being happy but like nobody wanted this except maybe Garrett #TheBachelorette"

"Even my dog is upset about what is happening right now #theBachelorette #TeamBlake"

"If Becca doesn't pick Blake, then BLAKE FOR BACHELOR..."

Thousands of tweets declared support for Blake. There was even a social media poll that asked "Did Becca make a huge mistake?" A USA Today headline questioned "Did Becca Choose the Wrong Guy?"

Through this sympathetic publicity, Blake suddenly found himself with fawning fans and social media clout. 2018 became the year life changed completely for both Blake and his mom. Suddenly, Shelly was immersed in the bizarre universe of reality TV, social media celebrity, image branding and screen stardom.

Fast forward to 2019. Oh, what a difference a year makes. Blake now appears on another broadcast in the Bachelor/Bachelorette franchise called "Bachelor in Paradise." And here's where Blake learns how quickly fame can turn sour. These are a few of the tweets from his stint on "Paradise":

"I know Blake sucks. I dislike him like everyone else."

"Get Blake the f$%# off my TV."

"Demi: 'Blake's a loser'
Jordan: 'Blake's a player'
Kristina: 'Blake's trouble'
WELLS: 'Blake's got problems'"

Ironically, the word "tweet" sounds innocent, but Blake's mom says the impact is far from it. The impact hit her personally when she watched social media cast its dark shadow over her son throughout the days of "*Paradise*."

"As a mom, it has been extremely painful to watch. And then to see how it has torn my son's entire life apart. He's not the same person he was before he went on that show." With pursed lips, Shelly described her son's panic attacks and a minor mental breakdown in those first days after "*Paradise*." "He doesn't trust anyone anymore. [He] feels like he's been stabbed in the back. He won't leave his house. He won't do anything. I actually had to take his phone away for a couple days for him to stay off of social media, because social media was so mean to him. It has just been the roughest thing I've ever been through."

Those rough days compelled Shelly to rise to the mothering challenge. At the height of social media trolls terrorizing Blake, Shelly "hid" him in her home for a week. Her greatest aim was to keep her son grounded in the midst of the media mayhem. "I had to explain to him and hope that he understood that this is very small. You may not think it's small, but it's small, very small. In the long run, something's gonna come out of it. And it did. He preaches about mental illness all the time now."

Blake agrees that one of his mom's best gifts to him during that difficult time was to keep him grounded and to help him recognize that good things come from hard times. "I look at it almost as a blessing in disguise. I've

Good things come from hard times.

been able to help a lot of people that I never would have been able to help before. I get DM'd a lot. I even had one the other day that was like, 'thank you, you saved my life. You talked openly about your struggles, so I was able to talk about my struggles and get therapy.'"

****

Blake's battle with the ruthlessness of reality TV was not unexpected. The year before, as Blake was wrapping up his initial *"Bachelorette"* season, I had asked Shelly how she felt about her son's newfound prominence. Surprisingly, even early on in the process, her mother's intuition detected a warning whiff of what was lurking behind the favor of fame:

> It's been difficult, it's been really difficult. Before, he was just kinda going along being the Blake he's been. Even though he had this unbelievable experience, when he comes home... it's still my Blake. He's going to work every day. He's doing what he's supposed to be doing. And then in the last, probably, six weeks, they've grabbed ahold of him and that famous Blake is starting to appear. We're not seeing him as much. He's traveling all the time. I'm trying really hard to keep him grounded as to who he is. He has asked his sister to keep him grounded. Because that's what America fell in love with, who Blake was, and how grounded and truthful and honest and genuine he was. And he needs to stay that way for America to still love him.

And there's the catch. Shelly immediately felt a burden to keep her son in the bubble of "who he was," so that America would approve. The madness of our media culture is this constant pressure to gain continual approval through followers, fans and "likes." And that pressure extends to moms. Not only did Shelly feel a need to maintain her son's approval from America, but she became aware of how her mothering influence had made that approval possible.

Shelly reflected on how her son's kind and unassuming personality had developed as a kid—under her guidance—in the years before their family was thrust into the spotlight. "In all of growing up, you can ask any of his teachers, he was a very, very quiet child. You'd have to call on him to get him to speak in class. He wasn't one to just speak out. He had tons and tons of friends, but never wanted to be that vocal person." Even as a quiet child, Blake attracted friends and perhaps, years later, maybe that translated into his ability to attract fans.

Was there a link between Blake's popularity and the way his mom raised him—the way she taught him to treat people? "I always wanted my kids to be respectful and that was either with their peers or with adults. I grew up that way. There was never any talking back. That wasn't gonna be allowed in my house. Your peers or your elders, you respect them. And I always made sure that my kids said 'please' and 'thank you' after everything."

Shelly's respect rules sprang from an underlying desire for her kids to practice kindness. "I think it was kindness more than anything. When my children asked for something, I wanted to make sure it came across that way, because they're asking, they weren't demanding."

The madness of our media culture is the constant pressure for continual approval.

Initially when her son became a celebrity, it seemed Shelly's mothering lessons had paid off. Published reports suggested that Blake was very well liked on *"The Bachelorette."* "There wasn't anyone that didn't get along with Blake. And I said, I would hope so because that's how he was brought up. He was nice to everybody. Even if he didn't like them, he was brought up to be kind to people. You don't need to bash people about something you don't like about them, their hairstyle or whatever it might be."

Those mothering lessons on kindness were pushed to their limit when Blake made his second run at winning the hand of a bachelorette on the show *"Bachelor in Paradise."* Suddenly, Blake's coveted "likes" began rapidly morphing into "haters."

****

From his very first episode on *"Paradise,"* Blake was the season's chosen villain. Admittedly, his villainous role was tied to some questionable personal choices. Before the contestants even landed in "paradise," Blake confessed to two of the bachelorettes that he'd slept with them on consecutive nights at a popular music festival known as Stagecoach.

Wait! Hold on!!! I know this isn't your typical mommy material. But it is the truth behind Shelly's story. And we can't learn the lessons of her mothering unless we dive deeper into her story. In this case, going deeper means getting into the misleading muck of reality TV.

After a televised "he said, she said" about their sordid sleeping arrangements, there were so many twisted truths and tall tales that the damage was already done. Blake had become the most hated bachelor in *"Paradise"* and social media followed suit. Shelly quickly discovered how the social media machine can drive a television show. "I think the social media part of it is what has created the show. You can't tell me that those producers don't go out and see what people are saying about their show... And so, the more tweets, the more posts that are out there about their show, they're doing their job."

Job well done? Blake was battered by hundreds of brutal social media attacks. "Within the first or second episode, he was a monster on that show. And that is not who he is." Shelly says Blake's friends shared her disbelief. "His sister had people send her text messages, like 'What is going on? This is not Blake.'"

That motivated Shelly to unearth a truth that's been cleverly buried since the dawn of television. The people who produce what's broadcast on our screens tend to live inside those screens, fully believing the "truth" they produce is reality. Worse, some of these puppet masters consider themselves superior to the millions of viewers they depend on who are glued to their screens.

I can make this claim because I personally witnessed the phenomenon when I worked in TV news. We'd regularly frame someone's tragedy to make it a salacious story for the screen. As producers of news, we sometimes cared more about the production than the reality. In the case of Blake and every other person who has been objectified on a screen, their produced lives became their real lives.

"This is real life. I know it's just television, but it's my life," Blake said quietly, holding his head in his hands, during one of his most painful *Paradise* episodes. Later, he wrote to his Instagram followers, "Never forget that we are all human and not characters on television."

Shelly expands on how Blake's real life was damaged by his TV one. "I raised Blake as a kind, gentle, honest person. The show created the Blake that did that at Stagecoach. The fame did that. That wasn't who I raised. The fame did that. Then the show tore him apart because of it, and they're the ones that created that."

Truthfully, the producers of "Paradise" were party to Blake's fame. And that fame was necessary. Without that notoriety, his humiliating fall wouldn't have held the potential to boost ratings. "The drama brings the ratings. The ratings make the money. And they don't care what happens along the way to anybody," Shelly asserts. "They manipulate it, totally manipulate it," referring to the producers' role in the relationships, the conflicts and, ultimately, the editing of the show.

You might argue that Blake did agree to let "The Bachelorette" portray him however they wanted while they were making him famous. You might also argue that producers shouldn't be held responsible for any wrong behavior on Blake's part. That's fair, but beyond a few bad decisions, Blake's mom claims he had very little control.

The truth is, when the house built by producers and publicists comes crashing down, there's very little the person inside the house can do about it. "They destroy them," Shelly says. "And I'm not even saying just Blake. There are other people that have been through hell and back because of this show. They're having the same issues Blake is. They're afraid to watch the show. They're afraid of what people are going to think about them."

She says this fear mindset was what caused Blake's mental health issues, and she speculates that the program might be detrimental to the emotional health of those who participate. She reveals that one person from ABC's extended staff recommended that Blake get professional treatment for PTSD after the "Paradise" taping was over.

Could this be an inadvertent confession that their programming has the potential to cause PTSD?

Maybe that's why Shelly had advised her son NOT to appear on "*Paradise*" when he was first asked. "I would tell people not to go on that show for anything. It's not worth the fame." She says that, although Blake never regretted his appearances on "*The Bachelorette*," he certainly regretted his decision to appear on "*Paradise*." And she gives us the reason for his regret in one sentence: "Because it destroyed him."

The destruction Blake went through is not a surprise to me. The risqué values behind "Bachelor nation" are a recipe for disaster. The show's format essentially calls for bachelors and bachelorettes to "test drive" multiple people in a short amount of time, sometimes getting intimate with several suitors back-to-back in the space of twenty-four hours. So, it's a little ironic that Blake was ridiculed for participating in the very behavior the show actually seems to promote—sleeping with two people on consecutive nights. The whole thing seems like a subtle form of prostitution.

With those destructive forces at work, Shelly says Blake became laser-focused on what people thought of him on social media, scrolling religiously through posts on his smart phone. "Blake wasn't upset about watching the TV show. He was upset about what people thought of him on social media." She points to direct hits that social media fired into her son's life: "Blake literally got DMs, direct messages from Instagram, people just tearing him apart and saying what a horrible person he is. They've never met the guy, but they feel the need, which blows my mind, to DM him directly."

"There was bullying." Shelly says, "With this day and age of school shootings and mass shootings, they are promoting bullying of people." The bullying went beyond condemning Blake's sleeping arrangements. Fellow "contestants" on "*Paradise*" actually began taunting him on the show. At one point, a group of bachelorettes snickered when Blake tore the entire toenail off his big toe while playing football on the beach.

Would we want social media to be judge and jury when our kids mess up?

Do you believe Blake's behavior justified public bullying? Based on moral or spiritual beliefs, most moms would probably say Blake's actions with the two women were very wrong. But won't our children make wrong choices of their own one day? Would we want social media to be judge and jury when our kids mess up? Probably not. Do we want our own child's phone-scrolling to become a daily dependency—as they constantly track what other people are saying about them? Shelly watched that scrolling-for-approval unfold in her own son's life. She was left to wonder if the combustible media of the 21st century would burn away any remnant of her careful mothering lessons and leave her son in the ashes left behind.

Would Shelly's mothering secrets be sacrificed on the altar of fame? Would Blake give up on his mom's rules of kindness and respect? Shelly hoped her parenting principles would prevail. And this is a universal "mom thing." Most moms work diligently to raise their babies well, so they don't want the world wreaking havoc on their work.

Put yourself in Shelly's shoes. Enter her early days—the days when she had big dreams as a mom, wanting the best for her children and having no inkling of what might threaten them one day. "Initially, when I went to college, I wanted to be a teacher, because I loved kids. So, I always knew, yes, I was gonna be a mom, no matter what."

That "no matter what" came along when Shelly was just twenty-three and Blake (her firstborn) came into the world. Shelly remembers feeling both excited and fearful. "I brought Blake home and it was scary. He wasn't an easy baby. I was just hoping to get through it. I was working at the time, so I took my three months off with Blake. And when I went back to work, it broke my heart."

Her broken heart led her to feel like a failure. "I wanted to be home with my first baby, but financially, at twenty-three years old, there was no way that was happening. I felt sick to my stomach. It was gut-wrenching to leave him. And he was screaming when I left him. He screamed every morning when I left him, until he was about a year old. Those were really tough, tough, tough days."

She confesses a burden shared with millions of moms—mother guilt. Ever felt it? I know I have. Shelly felt enormous guilt for taking her baby to daycare. "I didn't want someone else to raise him. I wanted to be the influence on him—his dad and I—not a babysitter that I'm paying money to every week. There was a lot of that guilt, of, no, I want it done this way, and will she treat him like I would, or bring him up like I would? Because she's with him eight to ten hours a day. That's a lot."

Many American moms feel like Shelly. Surveys show that a majority of moms admit they'd prefer to stay home with their kids, either part-time or full-time. Shelly was one of those moms—who yearn to be at home but know they can't afford not to work. As a result, she suffered pangs of mother guilt after the birth of Blake, and again three years later, when daughter Tori was born.

Although Shelly didn't get to spend her desired time at home, she carved out a daily routine that allowed her to be there for her kids. She secured a job in the local school system where her kids were educated, so she could see them during the school day. She explains that the concept of close-knit family—doing things together, going on family vacations and so on—was very important to her. "Family is number one in everything and anything you do, day in and day out."

Striving to hold up that family ideal is why she and her first husband fought to stay together when their marriage began to falter. "We were staying together for the kids. Make the kids happy. But I knew, they knew, they were not happy living in that kind of household, where there was screaming and yelling and fighting all the time. That was not healthy."

She surmises that she and her husband Rik would've been better off separating ten years earlier, in order to provide their kids some relief from their constant battles. "I felt that the divorce was for my kids too, because I didn't want them growing up into adulthood and going into a marriage themselves thinking this is okay. This is not okay. This is not normal. Screaming and yelling and slamming doors, that's not normal. That isn't what love is, and I didn't want them to think it was. And so, the divorce, yes, was partly for them. Yes, it was partly for me, because I needed my sanity back, but it was also for them."

Even though she argues that divorce was the best choice for her kids, Shelly admits that any hurt her kids felt before the divorce was probably matched by the hurt they felt after the divorce. She personally witnessed Blake's obvious pain after the divorce was underway. "He was helping me move into my apartment, and after we had moved the last load, he came out of the apartment and he was sitting on the deck stairs—just sitting there. And I walked up to him and asked, 'Are you okay?' And he goes, 'No' and he just started bawling." Shelly now begins to cry. Through tears, she remembers, "It finally hit him when I moved out—Oh my gosh, this is it. I won't have my family."

As Shelly revisits the sorrow of her divorce, I suggest that maybe there are two different kinds of pain for kids in these situations—first, the pre-divorce anxiety caused by parents visibly at odds and, second, the anguish caused by the disintegration of the family after divorce. Shelly observes, "I think the divorce pain was more of a sadness. You know, here we come upon our first Christmas. You're at Dad's one Christmas and you're at Mom's the next. There was a lot of that sadness for them, and I think sadness that we were not a family anymore."

Most of us know that divorce hurts kids. Studies prove it. The "separation" of divorce can cause collateral damage for kids caught in the middle. Since Shelly witnessed that damage firsthand, I ask if it caused her any regrets. "There are times that there is some regret on my part, where I think, why didn't I just stick it out? Or maybe we could've gone to counseling, and we could have changed this, or tried a little bit harder. Nineteen years we were married. And it was a long time. So, I look back and I think that, but I also think that there's a stigma to divorce that the kids have to deal with. It was a very hard decision for me to change my last name when I got remarried, because that is just another separation from my kids."

I confess that it's hard to write about another mom's divorce. Who am I to offer speculation about what's behind any woman's divorce? I'm deeply aware that divorce is not for bystanders to judge. Yes, there are damaging after-effects, but I'd rather hear from Shelly how she views the reverberations within her own family.

"I would say divorce is not ideal. It would be your last-ditch effort, because of the damage it can do to the kids, to the family. My kids have several sets of grandparents now, and that dynamic is totally different than if it's just your parents and his parents, and we're just one big happy family. If I was to give anybody advice, it's to see it as the last-ditch effort. You work through as much as you possibly can. And not to say that I'm not happy. I'm happy where I am and my kids are happy. They're happy [about] where I am and they will tell you that."

As Shelly surveys the silver linings in her divorce, she spots a hopeful glint—the struggle of separation was what forced her son to become a man. She believes Blake felt compelled to break out of his shell in order to protect his kid sister from any divorce fallout. "There, for a while, he and his sister got very, very close. He had to step up to be the man for his sister and be her voice. He was in high school. She was in middle school. It was hard for him to go off to college after that time, because he was going to be leaving her. So maybe that was also his way of growing up, and he just grew into this man. I mean, it was mind-blowing."

This was one of those "hands-off-the-steering-wheel" moments for Shelly. Don't you think every mom has these moments—when time seems to stand still and she's forced to step back from her daily parenting and watch how that parenting plays out in her child's choices? Shelly recalls the time it happened for her:

Blake came home his junior year and was just talkative, would talk to anybody. He could stand up in front of a crowd of hundreds of people and just talk. I remember looking at him, thinking, That's Blake? Because he was always so quiet and so shy. I think it really helped Blake to go to school in another state, where not all of his friends are. He knew no one when he went off to college, not a single soul. And coming from a small town and knowing everybody from kindergarten through twelfth grade, for him to pack up and go to another state, know no one, play football, find his own path, that's what it took. He was gonna have to do it. He was gonna have to branch out or he'd fail.

This more talkative persona came through on TV too, which surprised family and friends who knew Blake as a kid. Shelly says, "If you talk to any of his friends now, they say, 'I can't believe Blake was on TV, because the Blake I knew was very quiet and very shy.'" Blake's much more vocal personality on television led to greater exposure for his whole family—the kind of exposure his mom did not anticipate.

Again, Shelly's motherhood was put to the test when Blake progressed through various "cuts" on *The Bachelorette*." When he eventually became one of Becca's "Final Four," that's when producers set out to reveal more of Blake's personal life. He and his family were put under the media microscope, including Blake's past girlfriends, his high school, his small hometown, and even his parents' divorce, which was exposed on national television.

"There were times when they portrayed him on the screen and I'd go 'That's not true at all!' But that's how they wanted him to be portrayed, whether it be for ratings, whether it be for drama. I think you get molded in a way when you're on a screen. That's what social media does. It takes the little tiny piece and they run with it. Very insensitive. But there's actually people involved here, whether it be our divorce, whether it be Blake's old relationship with his ex-girlfriend, whatever it may be. It's not about anybody's feelings. It's what is best for them [the show]."

What ended up being "best" for the show was not best for Shelly. She was painfully surprised to hear her personal life laid bare on national television when Blake openly discussed the end of his parents' marriage. The discussion unfolded with Becca listening intently and the cameras looking on. Blake told Becca that he felt blindsided by his parent's divorce.

This is how it came out on TV: "For a long time we were the kind of family that brushes a lot of stuff under the rug. My parents got divorced when I was roughly a sophomore in high school. My mom fell in love with another man while still married to my dad. And that's hard enough, but it turned out the affair she was having was with my basketball coach and English teacher. And going through that in a small town makes it exponentially harder. So, I actually found out a lot through people in the community."

He then explained that one of those people was the first to let him know his mom was moving out. "I'll never forget one day a friend of mine came up and said, 'I heard your mom is moving into an apartment,' and I had no idea, like she knew before I did that my mom was moving out. So that's why this is so hard to kind of talk about, because my family didn't discuss it and that was really hard. So, if I've learned anything, it's that I want the openness in the family.

I don't want to raise my kids that way. I want to put family first over everything."

This televised speech exposed Shelly. Her private life now faced harsh scrutiny under a very public spotlight. She felt sure she'd be judged by hundreds of thousands of strangers. "They probably think I'm a sleazy whore to do that to my son, by having an affair (she makes quote gestures with her fingers) with his basketball coach, which wasn't very accurate. And Blake and I have since talked about this. I said, 'You know, Blake, I really wish that you would've come to me about this kind of information that you think you knew.'"

Off-camera, Blake explained to Shelly that he had described the divorce based on "talk" he'd heard from people in his rural home town of Bailey, Colorado. "This is the Bailey gossip. That's all he knew. I didn't know he knew this," Shelly exclaims, "until it came out on national television!"

I later asked Blake, in a separate interview, if he wanted it to come out the way it did on TV. "Unfortunately, this was probably the first time the editing really got to me, and I was really upset with ABC." He admits to saying what was broadcast, but also seems concerned that it may have appeared he was disrespecting his parents and their relationship. However, he holds the line on openness and reiterates that his biggest concern was his parents' lack of communication with him and his sister. "I had no idea what was going on. I had no idea. It kind of just happened all of a sudden."

I asked Blake if he thought his parents were trying to protect him by not talking about what was unfolding between them. He quickly answered, "Yeah, but I don't think that was necessarily the right thing."

Looking back, Shelly says she wishes her kids would have asked her questions. "I'd have been very honest with my kids, cuz I teach them to be very honest. There was never an affair. Mine and Dean's relationship was as very good friends. You can ask Rik. We all went out together. We were all just friends, all of us. Then, when my marriage—I say, 'started to fall apart,' no, it had fallen apart ten years earlier, but as I started going out and doing things as a group, I'm like, this is fun. When I go home, I'm miserable."

Both Blake and Tori told me, in follow-up interviews, that although they respect the fact that their parents tried to stay together for them, they've come to understand why their mom walked away from the marriage. Tori explains, "I think she always had our best interests at heart. I mean, she cared so much for us and wanted us to have the best life. I am so impressed how they did, and how they still can, put their differences aside and celebrate Blake and I and what we're doing and make sure that we're happy no matter what." Blake summed it up. "It obviously bothered my mom, me talking about it all.

[The town of] Bailey knows how much my mom loves me and my sister and how well she did raising us. It didn't change anyone's opinion in Bailey about my mom, but obviously with the world, it was a little different. I want them to know that people make mistakes. They're both so happy now apart. We had to go through those rough times. And I think it made us all stronger."

Rough times made this family stronger. But there's one rough time that we've saved for last. The rejection. A rejection that was magnified in the glare of the spotlight.

Shelly insists that her son had fallen in love with Bachelorette Becca and that he was hoping to be the bachelor she'd choose on national television. As the dramatic moment unfolded, Becca made her choice and millions of viewers witnessed her televised rejection of Blake's earnest marriage proposal.

That rejection scene was difficult to watch, especially for people who knew Blake. People like me. I've actually known Blake since he was a kid, because our family happens to live in Blake's hometown. In fact, Blake's sister Tori used to babysit our kids.

When Becca turned down Blake's proposal, our family had heartfelt reactions. Both my daughter and I cried as the scene unfolded.

And what a scene it was.

The last two bachelors standing are required to propose to the bachelorette. As the suspense builds, the TV audience waits to see which suitor she'll accept. So, there we were— our whole family watching our friend Blake, wearing his tailored suit in the blistering island sun, trying to brush away the sweat dripping from his brow, as he held Becca's hands and sincerely offered her his proposal of matrimony. She slowly responded with a dream-crushing "no."

The moment was heart-wrenching. Blake worked to keep his composure as he walked away from Becca, who stood waiting for the proposal that she would accept. Once he was a safe distance away, Blake's true emotions escaped. Millions of *Bachelorette* viewers got to watch Blake's tearful breakdown, as he stood all alone in a tropical forest, probably assuming the cameras couldn't "see" him there.

Shelly agonized over the hurt this caused her son. "He went through a horrible breakup on that show. He was truly, honestly, in love. People find that hard to believe, but if you were to ask him, yes, he was in love. He had a horrible heartbreak, and he felt like that was just tossed aside. It's chew you up and spit you out. There's no feeling for the human being that's standing there because that's not what it's about. It's not really about the person, it's about the drama."

Shelly insists that she and Tori nominated Blake for the show because of a genuine hope that Blake would find his wife and settle down. When that didn't happen, I wondered if Shelly thought putting Blake through the painful, public process was worth it. She assures me that it was, despite the pain, because of the people he was able to meet and the places he was able to see.

Add to that the fact that Blake became an official "influencer," which allowed him to be paid well for his new social status. An "influencer" is defined by Wikipedia as "someone (or something) with the power to affect the buying habits or quantifiable actions of others by uploading some form of original—often sponsored—content to social media platforms."

In the end, Shelly's story is a microcosmic study of the staggering force of social media and how it threatens modern moms and their kids. So many moms now have children who walk around with an extra appendage— namely, a six-by-three-inch screen. Every day, our kids glean image-driven values—or lack of them—from these smart devices. Often, kids learn more about the world from their phones than from their parents.

Smart screens threaten to turn us into a society of images, instead of a society of people. Image-branding often trumps the person behind the brand, as Shelly learned. "It's all about that image, and that's all they want you to see. They don't want

Smart screens threaten to turn us into a society of images instead of a society of people.

you to see that person behind it, because then it's not as dramatic or glamorous."

Are we teaching our kids that it's okay to sacrifice a person's feelings on the altar of entertainment? An altar packed with mean tweets, harsh memes and attacks from trolls who terrorize people?

Blake was an adult when social media mayhem threatened to tear his life apart. What about the young kids now being raised in the midst of this threat?

"If I was to go back and if I did see my kids at that age on social media, their heads are going to be messed up," Shelly says. "What they see and what they read can really mess with their life. You don't really know what your kids are on. You don't have any idea. It's so frustrating to me, because kids can be so mean to other kids. And I feel the same way. As my 30-year-old now, he's on this all the time, seeing what people are saying. It's just ugly. I would tell a mom, if you're going to let them be on that, I would monitor every single thing they go to."

Of course, Shelly's advice is backed by a mountain of research. Studies suggest that extensive use of smart phones and social media can make a child more prone to depression, anxiety, sleep deprivation, poor body image, bullying and suicide. Having seen these effects personally, Shelly advises moms not to hold back on limiting their child's smartphone usage and social media access. "Set limits," she says, because she knows that setting limits could literally save your child's life.

As for the rigors of reality TV, both Shelly and Tori have worked to keep Blake grounded in "actual reality." Shelly says this is her motherly duty. "You need to stay grounded, because you can't all get wrapped up in that fame. You need to keep that person, whether it be your daughter or your son, grounded. You have to stay grounded. You have to remember who you are, that you are a mom and you will always be a mom. You might be a mom to somebody who's famous, but you're still always mom and you have to remember that."

I would add my own two cents. It's my personal plea to moms like you: Please don't believe that somebody's importance on a screen translates to their importance in real life. I know "mom life" isn't glamorized on-screen, so you might think you're not as important as the latest Bachelorette or someone in the Kardashian clan. But that's modern media misleading you and me. The fact is that our screens overlook some of the most important people and most important positions on the planet. Like moms. Like you.

Shelly's motherhood did get some screen time when she played a cameo role in her son's TV life. Beyond the painful personal exposure for Shelly, there were some perks. People witnessed the results of her mothering as they watched Blake's behavior on-screen. Some viewers even reached out to compliment her. "I've gotten some emails, I've gotten some Facebook messages from people I don't even know, complimenting me on how I raised my children."

I'm almost relieved that she received this kind of feedback. I wish every mom could get a little publicity for the work she does to rear her children. But most moms go without publicity or applause. Sometimes a mom just needs to lean into the One who created her and her children—knowing that He sees her work and smiles.

As we conclude Shelly's saga of mothering in the twenty-first-century, I realize that almost every modern mom will face these same issues, including the prospect that her kids will be changed by the world. I suspect there are millions of moms who worry about how the culture will conflict with the lessons they've taught their kids. Shelly's been honest about exactly what kind of damage our culture can inflict. She pulled up a chair and gave us a front-row seat.

Shelly left us with good reasons to insist on teaching our kids kindness and respect, even when those things are hard to come by. Maybe especially when those things are hard to come by. She taught us that a mother's love must shine above the fray as a guiding light in a surreal, digital world that can be very, very dark.

Shelly's Amazing Mom Secret:
Overcome social media negativity by teaching your kids kindness and respect.

Why **You** Are Amazing #3:
(re-read often)

You wield the power to influence your child more than any influencer. As a mom, you offer protection to your child by limiting who can have access to their priceless heart. You are your child's champion when you shelter them from unhealthy internet access, social media and cyber bullies.

Chapter 4
Fostering Greatness
Linda Wesselin

Just days after giving birth to her first baby, she
walked away from her first husband. It was about
protection. After protecting her firstborn, Linda hasn't
stopped protecting children since—more than one
hundred children. As a foster mom, she's seen what's
gone wrong for children, for mothers, for families in
America. And she boldly points out the greatest threat
to the modern family.

✳✳✳✳✳✳

She is an expert on families gone bad. She's lived it. She's studied it. She's opened her whole heart to it, by caring for the kids who are its victims. If you want to know the greatest threat to modern families, Linda Wesselin will tell you.

Linda is a foster mom. She's fostered one hundred and three children. Yes. ONE. ZERO. THREE.

Linda is a mom who filled in for other moms when their mothering failed. She knows something about what makes motherhood fail or succeed. Motherhood—at its worst and at its best.

Linda has horrific stories that include things like iron burns on the backs of babies. But she also has hopeful stories of kids whose love for their parents never dies.

Linda has "seen it all" when it comes to family. She's had to pick up the broken pieces of dysfunction and mend the wounded hearts left behind. She's observed unmistakable patterns and terrible tendencies. She's been unwittingly sucked into the continual wake of broken families—a wake that surges from one generation to the next.

To Linda, the "crisis of family" is not a political talking point. It's not hilarious subject matter for TV sitcoms. It's not something government programs can repair with enough funding. And it's not an issue we can sweep under the rug without dire consequences for the future of humanity.

Linda has the "inside story" on why families fall apart and how it can be avoided. This is the beacon of hope in Linda's story. She's confident that she can identify the root of the family breakdown. She can tell us which habits must be nipped in the bud. As she witnessed what made families become unwell, she's blazed a trail for every mom who wants to do family well. In fact, Linda may have the mothering secret that could fix millions of families.

One of the best things about Linda's case study is that she's lived it from both sides. While working with the most alarming cases of dysfunctional families, Linda raised three children of her own within a functional family. With her husband, Jerry, she figured out how to do family well while observing the unwell. She brings the full gamut of experience to her ideas about motherhood, including a very personal setback in her own mothering story.

Linda began motherhood as a single mom. Just days after the birth of her first child, Linda realized her new family was on a dangerous path toward dysfunction. "Not everybody has the perfect husband. I didn't either. And I recognized that early on. Tiffany was three days old when I walked out, and I walked out with the clothes on my back and every baby thing I could pack in my car."

What would make her leave the father of her child just days after their daughter's birth? Linda says she simply realized he wasn't going to be a good dad. "I don't know why it took three days after bringing her home to figure that out, but, man, that hit me like a ton of bricks. And I just said, this is bad and I'm not doing it. It was so bad all of a sudden. When I figured that out, I knew that whatever I could provide for her on my own was better than what I had there. That's how bad that was."

As a single mom, Linda vowed to protect her daughter Tiffany. She made a steadfast rule that no man would ever come before her daughter. "I didn't make every man that I met a priority over Tiffany. When I found Jerry, it was very carefully plotted and planned how to fit Jerry into my family, because Tiffany still had to come first. I didn't know who he was and I wasn't going to let him be in that number one position. I already had Tiffany, so he was coming in afterwards. I wasn't going to move her down to move him in, because who knew how that was going to work out? That's not how the women today are, however."

Linda steps up to her soapbox and makes her case, a case that's been building over nearly 25 years of fostering kids. No research study. No scientific analysis. Just caring for wayward kids. This is what brought Linda to one, specific conclusion. She claims it's the most damaging trend within modern families. The trend of missing fathers.

Pointing a finger at absentee dads is certainly not new. Maybe that's why Linda is more concerned about how moms respond to the problem of AWOL dads. She claims that, without the father around, the mom will seek some kind of replacement, whether it's a boyfriend, a drink, a drug or a distraction: "A lot of kids come into foster care now because the moms are more interested in the boyfriends than they are in taking care of the kids, so the kids get neglected. We had a daughter towards the end, in 2012, whose mother and grandmother pimped them out to boyfriends for drugs. Her and her sister."

These "pimped" girls were just eleven and thirteen years old at the time. Linda says these kinds of horrific scenarios can often be blamed on the fact that fathers are missing. However, the problem is not solved only by blaming deadbeat dads.

Linda points out that dads are missing partly because they're no longer valued by our culture. Interestingly, she thinks the fathering job is devalued both by fathers and mothers, but almost never by children. Linda goes so far as to blame the low value placed on dads for the majority of modern family dysfunction:

> The kids get moved clear to the bottom of the pile, because other men and drugs and alcohol come

before the children now. The priority is the next drink or the next can of beer or the next drug fix or the next boyfriend or the next night out to find the next boyfriend, and the kids are left who knows where with who knows what and who knows what resources to survive. I think that's a lot of what is wrong. This gets a little biblical, honestly, but it takes a mom and a dad to have a kid, and there's a reason that happens. They both play unique roles, and if you want your kids to be successful and whole and complete, it takes the two pieces. Not that there aren't great single moms out there.

In fact, Linda has great sympathy and respect for single moms, partly because she's been one. She acknowledges the brave women thrown into the single-mom category, due to abuse, addiction, abandonment or the death of their child's father. She applauds the dedicated single moms who've created exceptions to the dysfunctional, fatherless-family rule.

Still, the existence of successful, single moms doesn't diminish the incalculable importance of dads. Children need fathers, and children need mothers to pick fathers who will last. Any one part subtracted from the family total can cause dysfunction.

"I think it's about family values. It's not just being a mom. I think there's a reason there's a dad. It's about family. It's not about being a single mom. There are great single moms, but if you have a choice, it's much better to have children being raised with moms and dads."

What about the fact that Linda chose the very circumstance she warns against? You'll recall that she chose a "daddyless" family for her baby girl. Despite this, she adamantly defends the role of fatherhood as key to the success of family and children. Maybe that's partly because she and her second husband have dedicated most of their fostering years to filling the dad-shaped void in their foster kids' lives.

"I think the thing that we saw the most was, almost every foster kid that came into our care was from a single mom. And the problem with [these] single moms was that they had a boyfriend who became the priority. Then you have the moms that play 'who's your daddy?' They've got six paternity tests and still haven't found the right dad. So, we've got kids growing up with 'who's your daddy?' and they just do the same thing they've seen somebody else do. So now we have it multi-generationally stacked, and we saw that in foster care."

We've entered the era of single parents, with nearly 40% of children born out of wedlock.

She says that the syndrome repeats itself, growing to greater and greater proportions over time. Research confirms that we've entered the era of single parents, with nearly 40 percent of children being born out of wedlock and tens of millions of children growing up without a dad in the home.

Kids with missing fathers are significantly more likely to be poor, to drop out of school, to commit crimes, to go to jail, and to have suicidal thoughts. They're also more likely to replicate the fatherless homes they came from when they have families themselves. These chronic problems are tied to the family, or lack of family, in a child's life.

Linda points to the ghosts of relationships that follow kids into foster homes and beyond. "When you bring in a foster kid, not only do you bring in that child, you bring in their mom, their dad, their aunt, their uncle, the grandma, the grandpa, the brother, the sister. And sometimes you do get brothers and sisters, physically. So, you bring in a kid that's a whole lot of everybody. You don't deal just with that child. You deal with the whole family. There can be a whole lot of brokenness in that."

Brokenness manifests in multiple ways, from physical appearance to emotional and behavioral issues. Linda recalls one of the most horrific physical cases. "We had the kid who had the marks of an iron in the middle of his back where he had been burned."

Linda has a memory bank of scars, which includes numerous tales of child abuse. She recalls another case that involved extreme mental anguish for two girls "who watched their grandmothers overdose on drugs that were sold to them by their moms' boyfriends."

Then Linda points her finger at another controversial cause—a cause I wasn't sure I should share in this book. I was concerned it might make you slap the book shut forever. Still, I've included Linda's bold opinion because its merit is based squarely on her extensive experience. Linda doesn't hold back, "I blame it on birth control. When it got to the birth-control piece, you could cheat. [Indiscriminate sex] didn't matter, because you could cheat and maybe not get caught, because you weren't having babies."

I understand Linda's point. It's true that we're now in an era in which a man or woman can practice "safe sex" without factoring in the natural outcome of sex—new life. It's true that, unlike any other time in human history, we can commit the one act that creates life and effectively detach that act from the creation of life. Sex for the sake of sex. Life subtracted. Because of birth control.

Women no longer have to be dependent on men. They can separate sexual intimacy from commitment, from marriage, from babies, and from family. Linda says, "I think we've come to accept it. I think there's a level of acceptance, because there's so much of it out there that you think, what are you gonna do and what can you say? And now it's multi-generational. As soon as we had birth control, you could cheat."

We are now wandering into politically incorrect territory. I know millions of women equate birth control with the right to choose what they do with their bodies. And, of course, the great majority of women in western culture rely greatly on birth control; it's considered an indispensable component of sexual reproduction. But I would argue that Linda is tapping into an important question. Has birth control, in subtle ways, diminished the value we place on life, on family, and on motherhood itself?

Besides the opportunity to cheat, Linda says, "you get the problem with the birth control that didn't work, and then you have the first generation of kids that came along because the birth control thing didn't work." The result is unwanted children, yet another sign of the diminished value placed on individual lives. In fact, the "unwanted" status of many children has laid the groundwork for foster care.

Whatever your personal view of birth control or abortion or healthy family design, Linda's foster care experience does point to a family crisis that no one can deny. Through our new ability to manipulate conception, fetal development and birth, the necessity of dads has been diminished. Dads have been subtracted from the family structure in millions and millions of families. The sorry result of that steady subtraction is a disintegration of family in our modern culture. And the end game of that disintegration is broken children left behind.

Linda brings up another aspect of broken children that presents a troubling predicament for the foster parent: the child's broken heart. Linda theorizes that a foster child's mangled heart makes it very hard for that child to receive love, especially from a foster parent.

If you're a parent to biological children, you may take the reciprocal nature of parental love for granted. You give love to your children and you receive love back. Imagine, however, if you loved on your kids every moment of every day, and those beloved children were incapable of receiving and returning your love.

If you are a foster or adoptive parent, you probably understand what Linda's describing. Linda has lived through this rejection cycle repeatedly.

"Parenting foster kids is very different, and I learned that over the years. It took many years for me to realize what I was doing wrong and what was not okay. You don't learn it overnight and it didn't come quickly. There are no books out there to say this is how to parent a foster kid. I think it's true that every parent that goes into foster parenting thinks that they're going to foster kids like they parent their own. You can try to do it, but you will always be on the losing end emotionally."

Linda confesses her slow learning curve as a foster parent. In the early days, she found herself struggling to show her first foster child unlimited love.

"It doesn't work, because she's not going to receive it. When it's not received, there's no giving back, and then you're just feeding this empty soul.

It's true when you parent, you want something back. We all do. And I think that's normal. I think it's true that when we parent our kids, we love them dearly. We know they're gonna love us back so you're not just feeding this emptiness. You do get things back. Our kids get through school and they learn to read, and we get to smile and laugh, because they're giving us back information all the time and they're able to do that because we give to them."

Perhaps I'm a spoiled mom. Or maybe I'm a bit selfish in the way I love my kids, because when Linda admits that she loved her foster children without getting any love in return, I'm flabbergasted. I sheepishly confess that I rely on getting a little love, or affection, or at least a "thank you" every now and then to prop me up in my mothering.

My own kids naturally give me that kind of love in return. I don't demand it. I don't force it. Frankly, I probably wouldn't stop loving my kids even if they decided to stop loving me back. A mother's love is fairly indestructible, even when we don't always get the love we desire in return. However, I see the role of foster parent as uniquely sacrificial. Foster parents love kids through horrific circumstances and hurtful behaviors with little expectation of receiving love in return. Although certainly there are exceptions, Linda insists that these kids are unable to return the foster parents' love because they lack foundational love:

> You look at kids as needing a foundation to be built on. Foster kids don't get the proper foundation from day one, which is, when babies cry, they need to be

A mother's love is fairly indesctructible.

picked up so they know they're worth being picked up. They know you're going to be there and they know that you care enough to pick them up when they're crying. Those foundational blocks start when they're infants.

A lot of parents whose kids end up in foster care don't do all that foundational building from day one. Babies cry too long; they don't ever get picked up; they're not really nurtured. You'll see a lot of young moms sometimes feeding their babies, and they'll have the bottle in the mouth, and they're watching TV and never have eye contact with their babies. Those things are all really important, and foster kids tend to miss all that stuff.

When they're finally pulled from their home and get stuck into a home where you want to be a mom, they don't know how to handle all that. When you look at them and you're having a conversation with them, and you're telling them they matter and it's important for them to get their homework done, it just goes nowhere, because they've got nothing to build on that says, "I do matter. It is okay." Parenting foster kids is entirely different than parenting biological kids. You have to look at it differently.

Linda admits that the fostering learning curve was a slow climb for both her and her husband Jerry:

I think Jerry and I loved every kid that came in our door. We absolutely did the best that we could do... I don't think we knew that it was going to be different with foster kids than it was with our bio kids. We just thought they were kids and, if we treat them all the same, they'll all be the same. It took us a while, and I'm kind of a slow learner for sure.

It took me a while to learn they're not going to treat us the same. But we still loved them and did what we needed to do, because we always kind of believed until the last day we did foster care, somebody will come back someday and tell us that if it hadn't been for something that we did with them, their lives would be different. Whether it's that they sit down and eat dinner every day as a family themselves now, because that's what we did or... We just never knew what was going to be the one piece that they would take away and make them be a better adult.

To date, Linda doesn't remember any of her foster kids returning to her home to report the happy results of the foster care she and her husband provided. But the love of a mother remains in her heart. She is still waiting for one of her 103 to walk back through her door and say, "Thanks for being my mom."

It took us so long to learn that we were never going to get anything back, because every time a kid left and then you got the new one, you thought, OK, I'll make these changes and maybe it'll help and I'll get something back. Your whole career you're making changes and you're doing things differently and you're trying to refine it, because you're like, one of these kids someday is gonna love me too. And they just don't. It never happened.

Sometimes there's a bond and it starts to work, but that's when they freak out, because they have attachment issues. Then you've got to pull back, because it's too much for them. You're pulling back and then they get comfortable again. Then you're like, oh this is really cool, I love this kid. So you move in again and they kind of freak out. It's a game. It's a game, because you want to love on them and let them know that they're loved and yet they can't always handle that.

I pause to compliment Linda, hoping to give her a little of the recognition she never received from her foster kids. I tell her that, for those twenty-four years of foster care, she was honing the art of true love. To me, "true love" is to love someone without getting anything in return. Linda can only respond with a modest "yeah."

Linda's not one to dwell on her own commendable behavior. She seems to know it was her calling to serve as "mom" to so many, even without love in return or success on paper.

Linda's also not one to complain about her disappointments as a foster mom. It's more like she's educating than complaining. The education continues as she schools me on another foster care topic—the persistence of what we might call "original love." Linda explains that most foster children, no matter how poorly they've been treated by their biological parents, still feel love for their original mom and dad.

"It didn't matter what the abuse was or how bad the neglect was or how awful the home was or how bad the environment was. The one common piece that every kid in our home came with was they just wanted to go home and be loved by their mom and dad, if they knew who they were."

The steadfast love of children for parents whose blood they share is a "let-bygones-be-bygones, never-say-never" kind of love. I asked Linda if this kind of diehard love existed in the child with iron burn marks on his back, left there by his mom. "Oh yeah! He told me, 'You're not my mom. You will never be my mom and I'm just gonna go home. I wanna be with my mom.'" She explains that abused children like this boy would often justify their biological parents' behavior to her. "He says, 'It could have been worse.' I cannot tell you how many kids have sat in our home and said, 'It's really not that bad.'"

Revealing my faith in the goodness of God's creation, I observe that maybe He creates children to automatically love the mothers who give birth to them. Linda seconds my observation. "I'm just saying, if the moms would figure out how to get the priority piece right, these kids would love them back. If the kids were the priority and it wasn't the next drug or the next drink or the next boyfriend. If it really was that kid, what an amazing relationship all these moms could have with their kids. The kids are willing. The kids are there. The kids want to be loved, but they want to be loved by their parents, not some home they got dumped into."

Linda has faith in the raw potential of motherhood and family despite the endless dysfunction she's witnessed — dysfunction that infected her own nuclear family. Linda admits that her offspring were affected by having to share their parents with over a hundred other children, many of whom were deeply troubled. Linda's two oldest children, Tiffany and Brandon, were immersed in the foster care lifestyle when they were very young.

Tiffany was six and Brandon was an infant when Linda got the urge to start "paying it forward." She explains, "It really stemmed from giving back. When my son was born, he was really sick. We were in a little apartment and I was a stay-at-home mom to Tiffany. Jerry was the only one working, and we lived in this just awful, awful apartment. My grandpa helped us buy our house, which was really big of him. The one thing I knew how to do was be a mom, so foster parenting was a place that I could give back for what we'd been given."

Tears begin to well up in Linda's eyes as she remembers her grandfather's generous gift at a very difficult time. That one, single gift seems to have inspired Linda's life philosophy, because it introduced her to a model of giving back through foster care.

"We paid it forward, not knowing even what that was, before it was ever even a thing. You know, people didn't think about paying it forward in those terms. There weren't just random acts of kindness. We were just blessed to have a house and to be able to have a place to raise our kids, and we didn't need all the rooms. It was something I could do from home that didn't interfere with Jerry. He could do his job and it would be my job. It was something that I could do while I was staying home raising my family."

Linda says her two oldest kids came through the process with more appreciation than resentment. Tiffany has already served as a foster parent while raising two of her own children, and Brandon has expressed an interest in fostering as well.

Linda's youngest son, Tim, has a different take. He struggles with the dysfunction that seeped into his childhood. "Tim is the one that's most resentful. He saw the worst and he was the youngest. When we look at some of the foster kids that we lived with way longer than we should have, Tim was the one who was in his most important years when those kids were in our home. Emotionally, on some levels, and intellectually, we probably did some damage to Tim by keeping some kids too long, because I just don't give up. I'm kind of a fighter."

This fighter of a foster mom says she couldn't help herself. She kept insisting that her relentless mother love would change something for each kid who walked through her door. She was determined to fill that gaping parent void. But her youngest came to resent the open-door policy, which allowed other kids to share his parents.

Linda admits, even as a young adult, Tim still expresses displeasure over the foster kids who imposed on his childhood. Linda's face reveals heartache when she talks about her son's resentment of her fostering, but she holds onto hope, the hope that Tim knew his parents were trying to do right by the kids they fostered.

"He knows that, but he's not going to go out and do foster care. When we have family conversations about it, he's the one that will have the ugliness to throw in the pot." Despite Tim's disapproval, I wonder how Linda feels about how her own kids turned out after her foster care journey. What was the aftermath—if any—of having a mom who was focused on 103 other kids?

My daughter's a stay-at-home mom, and I have the three most amazing grandkids that she and her husband are raising. She's an over-the-top, ridiculous mom. Some days I think, what are you doing? But, you know, I'm kind of over the top, too. The apple didn't fall far from the tree. She's a great mom and she had the ability to find an amazing husband. She finished school. She didn't have babies before she left school. She was married before she had babies, so I feel really good about that. And we don't have drug and alcohol problems in our family. I feel really good about that.

Brandon didn't have children before he was married. Both of my boys are electrical engineers and finished college, and they work hard. I just love my family. I am blessed. I get that I couldn't have done that all on my own, but we worked hard to have the kids that we have. It didn't come easy. I'm glad they were receptive to what we did for them, because you can have great and amazing parents who don't always end up with great and amazing kids. It's not always about the parenting. There's some free will in there from the kids. I think we've been blessed that our kids have chosen good stuff.

As Linda celebrates the more positive outcomes of her motherhood, I ask what mothering secret she's discovered in the midst of it. I'm deeply aware that Linda's secret will be unique because of the kinds of kids she has mothered. She's had to come up with her very best, in order to fix the very worst in foster children. So, not surprisingly, Linda's mothering secret goes back to the kids. Kids as the priority. Every parent needs to make their kids a top priority.

"I don't have a six-figure income, we don't live in a big house, we don't live in a fancy neighborhood, we don't drive big cars. It's all about the priorities and where you put the kids. If your priority is to have a six-figure income and a big house and be a size 2, then I'm going to say your kids were not a priority. You made those other things your priority, and you've already got it all wrong. You're not generally going to end up with a great and amazing kid, because you didn't have the priorities in the right place. The baby comes first, bottom line. If your babies don't come first, you're in trouble and your babies are gonna be in trouble."

I ask Linda to clarify a few things. Is she saying our kids should be treated like royalty, viewing themselves as the center of the universe? I think a lot of us would be opposed to letting our kids believe they're the "little gods" of our households. Linda quickly acknowledges that children need to learn humility even when parents make them a top priority.

I also wonder if Linda is implying that a mom can only make her children a top priority by refusing to take a job outside the home:

> I'm not saying you can't have a career, but if you don't get the kids in that first priority place, no matter what your career, that's when the problems start. Where people tend to get that twisted up is when they have a career, and the career becomes more important and the kids get pushed down.

> It happens kind of slowly, I think, so you don't recognize that your priorities have moved positions a little bit. Maybe your boss says, "I need you to stay for an extra hour tonight just to get this one deadline thing done," and maybe it was Johnny's swim meet that you didn't get to go to, but auntie got to go. Can you justify it in your head: well, it was good for auntie to get to do that? Little things like that start to creep in and, before you know it, things get rearranged and those priorities get twisted.

Linda would tell you that all her kids were a top priority. For the final "proof in the pudding," I look again to Linda's biological children. In my brief time with Linda, it appeared her grown children still want to hang out with their mom and dad. Tim walked through the living room several times, even as Linda and I were talking. Brandon's family stops in often, as Linda cares for one of their children during the week. Tiffany and Brandon are proving that "imitation is the highest form of flattery," as they both have considered parenting kids in foster care, just like their mom and dad:

> I just know that we did enough of the right things. I'm not saying we did it all right. Lord knows, there's a learning curve, so I'm sure there are things that we didn't do right. But I know that we did enough right that every kid that left our house took something out of here they will use some day, and that is faith. That is absolutely faith-based. And I think the kids that we had later on in our career that were the more difficult kids, even though those kids were harder, we got better as foster parents. I think those are the kids that truly stand a better chance of having something to take away from what we've done.

Finally, I ask Linda what motherhood, in total, means to her. This humble mother of 106 answers as only she could: "I wouldn't know what else to do."

Linda's Amazing Mom Secret:
Make your kids a top priority.

Why **You** Are Amazing #4
(re-read often)

You are giving your children the best start in life simply by being present. As you choose to show up, to keep your word—to watch, watch and watch again—your kids feel your love through your reliable presence. As you're asked to applaud for the 50th cartwheel or sit through the 100th athletic event or, perhaps, the 20th awards ceremony, your kids will be emboldened by the fact that their mom is there. Putting them first.

Chapter 5
Having It All
Gretchen Carlson

Her famous face doesn't reveal the pain she has suffered privately. The doctor's call that reduced her to tears. The debilitating condition that threatened her baby. The internal struggles during her very public sexual harassment case. You're about to get the inside scoop. Gretchen Carlson drops her stoic TV anchor persona to share her real-mom feelings in the midst of some real-life struggles.

******

As you read through the first words of this chapter, you might wonder what a famous, wealthy, powerful woman like Gretchen Carlson could possibly have in common with you. How could she identify with your struggles, understand your hardships, or speak to your parenting woes? It's a good question, because Gretchen's public persona can be intimidating. A high achiever, she's big on accomplishments and small on visible flaws. She sports a classic, Minnesota stiff upper lip that never quivers. In public. But Gretchen has experienced trials that speak to the life of a typical mom— even if she's anything but typical. She understands the challenges of mothering. And she hopes her larger-than-life story encourages moms like you to pursue your dreams, despite setbacks and hardships.

Gretchen is a woman who pursued her dreams and reached them. Because of that, she may look like she's got it all. Pretty. Smart. Famous. Successful. Good marriage. Healthy children. But that description doesn't paint a complete picture. Like a lot of moms, Gretchen has experienced personal pain, although her pain has remained outside of the public's view.

For starters, there's Gretchen's childhood, which was marred by merciless teasing. She says the rejection stemmed from the fact that she was a "chubby" girl who played the violin—a recipe for negative attention in the small Minnesota town where she grew up. Years later, as a high-profile TV personality, she battled adult versions of those same trials, enduring ruthless critics, sexist bosses, petty putdowns and mean tweets.

In light of her trials, Gretchen declares you just "can't have it all." In fact, she made that line famous in the 1989 Miss America Pageant when she answered one judge's question. "I was the only person at the pageant to answer that interview question in that way. And I certainly didn't mean that women shouldn't strive for their very best, but let's just be honest about the whole thing."

Gretchen urges women to let go of that false ideal that they should have it all. "I feel like women feeling guilty that they're supposed to have it all, it's a curse. We're never going to live up to that. And so, when I'm working, I'm giving work 110%, but then I'm not giving my kids 110%. But when I come home—sorry to tell you, I'm checking in with work a little bit, but I am in the moment with my kids."

Having kids was a goal for Gretchen from the time she was little. She recalls the exact moment when the desire to have babies was etched on her soul. "I remember having pneumonia when I was about five years old and being in the hospital, and the nurses coming in and picking me up so I could see all the babies in the window next to me, and ever since that day I wanted to have kids."

This is a surprising announcement from a woman famous for announcing the news. Gretchen's determination to be a mom appears out of place in a world that doesn't expect high-achieving women to dream of raising babies. Author Julie Roys sums up that idea, claiming that in the 21st century, science, politics, and popular culture have worked together to suggest that motherhood is "insignificant" and that "devoting oneself to motherhood is somehow insufficient."

Personally, I've noticed a subtle devaluation of motherhood, even as I've worked at ChannelMom to champion the role of moms. I've known moms who were ridiculed at shopping malls because they had "too many" kids. I've met moms who felt forgotten when they left their careers to raise their kids at home. And I've heard from moms who felt like their "professional job" was far more respected than their mothering job.

One acquaintance even relayed a story to me about a speaking tour she did, aimed at kids in high school. She said, almost without fail, when she'd ask the audience of students what they wanted to do when they grew up, there would be a group of girls who remained silent. According to this woman, those girls were afraid to admit that they wanted to be moms.

I wonder out loud to Gretchen if our modern media is to blame. Does the media imply that mothering is not a cool job? Do we leave girls feeling that being a mom is a fast track to irrelevance? Are we glorifying the latest Hollywood celebrity or the sports hero at the expense of moms? When our kids look at their screens, do they ever see motherhood as a desirable role? Gretchen ponders these questions and finds answers in her own family heritage:

> The first thing that comes to mind for me are the amazing moms I had in my life. My grandmoms were amazing, trailblazing women, who didn't work [outside the home], but one grandmother traveled the world after her husband died. And I thought, wow, she was really pushing the envelope. And my other grandmother was the one who played the violin and just taught me so much about relationships and how to be kind to other people.

> My own mom, of course...she was my main inspiration for my drive. She told me every night when she put me to bed after prayers, "You can be anything you want to be, Gretchen." I believed her. I knew I had to work hard to get there, but she

believed in me. And she was a stay-at-home mom, this amazing woman who's raising four kids and volunteering and teaching Sunday School and singing in the church choir. Just a wonder woman in my mind, even though she didn't work outside the home. And she raised me to be able to do anything that I possibly could in life. So, to me, that's a testament of how powerful moms are. Now she's turned her whole life around, now that all the kids are gone. She's now CEO of a company at 75.

She's now doing what maybe she should have been arguably doing, but thank goodness, for my benefit and my siblings' benefit, she was with us. The biggest part of that was not only the time commitment, but the messaging: Building my self-confidence and making me feel, even when I was fat as a kid, even when I didn't win the violin competition, even when I didn't make Student Council, even when I didn't make the school play, building me up to say, "You can still be whatever you want to be in life." I think about that every single night and I'm passing that along to my children.

Gretchen's testament to the moms in her life is a reminder of the powerful impact moms can have. Still, Gretchen is aware that society may not echo her opinion. During her years of reporting the news, she admits she witnessed subtle suggestions that women don't need to value the mom role

My career doesn't matter to me if I cannot have kids.

and that greater value should be placed on women who work outside the home.

A personal battle with infertility might be one reason Gretchen sees motherhood as something of priceless value:

> I never ever, ever, ever in my wildest dreams thought that I would battle infertility. I started trying to get pregnant when I was thirty-five and thought, well, this isn't too late. My mom had four kids and it was never an issue. And it was just so mind-boggling that day when I found out it's going to be a tough road for me. I remember calling my mom, sitting on a bench near Central Park, sobbing my eyes out and saying, "Mom, this will be my greatest disappointment in life if I cannot have children. My career doesn't matter to me if I cannot have kids."

Like many women who dream of having a family, Gretchen felt despair over that infertility diagnosis:

> I think what made me so despondent on that first day is that the fertility doctor said to me on that very first meeting, "You have a 3-percent chance of getting pregnant by yourself. Have you ever thought about a donor egg?" I didn't even know what a donor egg was! Until you start going through fertility issues, you're not schooled on that kind of stuff. But to tell me right away, in the first meeting, to suggest that the baby would be somebody else's, it just came as such a shock. [I] never thought it would be me. Never envisioned it at all. Never even considered it. Then to hear that it would be somebody else's baby with my husband. It was hard to wrap [my mind]

around. But then, soon after, I just decided, okay, like anything else in my life that I've struggled with, how am I going take this on?

She began to see her problem in light of her TV news audience and the great likelihood that many of them had experienced the same infertility anguish:

> It's a silent pain that many couples go through. You feel a sense of shame, because it's your own body. It's like, well, why are my eggs bad? Or why is my sperm bad? Or whatever. So, couples struggle with this in silence together. It's not something that you go to work and [say] "Hey, I can't have a baby." So, there's that. And then, also, I wanted to talk about it, because I think doctors should give the real story a lot earlier than [age] thirty-five.

> I'd never seen that chart where your fertility just does this [her hand motions down] after thirty... There are a bunch of people out there who think that they can be forty-five and have a baby and it will be their own. I just feel like we should have a reality check and be honest with our women. Not to say, "Hey, you should get pregnant at twenty-five," but, "Here are the realities of it and here's the chart," just so women are more educated about it.

Even though infertility took a toll on her emotions, Gretchen reveals that her most emotional moment came after she became a mom—after her infertility issues, after her pregnancy, and after giving birth to her first child, Kaia.

"It was finding out that my three-month-old first baby, my daughter—after struggling to have her—that she had a tumor in her eye and that she might go blind. I remember being on the phone with my mother. I was so upset about it that she got on an airplane and came out to New York City that day to be with me, because we had some crucial decisions to make about her [the baby's] health.... there wasn't an easy decision or cure for the condition that she had. I would say that was probably the most emotional time for us as parents."

Their emotions were tested further when the cure for their baby was almost as bad as the condition:

> We ended up having a drug to give her that was very controversial. I had to give it to her every morning. She would be looking up at me, smiling and kicking her legs, and I knew I was feeding her poison. And I would cry. Tears would be streaming down my face as I was looking at her and she was smiling at me, and I was feeding her the poison. I mean, it was poison because it potentially had lifelong side-effects, but, in the short run, it was going to decrease this tumor. So, you know, we make tough choices in life. And that one was just the most emotional, because I was so overjoyed to finally be having a baby and then to find out, so soon after, that she had this incredibly serious condition.

As it turned out, the medicine did not leave Kaia with any lasting or devastating side-effects. However, it did leave Gretchen with yet another reason to appreciate the gift of motherhood.

As we ponder that gift together, I bring up the story of Kara Tippetts (Chapter 8). Like Gretchen, Kara placed a high value on mothering. As a mom in her thirties, battling terminal cancer, Kara insisted on loving her children "BIG" until the moment she died. Not long before her death, Kara said, "So often, as moms, we're waiting for the promotion, the next house, the vacation, and we struggle to live present in our moments with our families." Facing death taught Kara to slow down and appreciate her family moments as precious. I wonder how Gretchen perceives the value of motherhood when she thinks of somebody like Kara, who didn't get to "finish" her time with her family:

> Well, first of all, that's absolutely tragic. I can't imagine the kids left behind or Kara looking down from heaven. I don't like to be a fatalist, but I often think about what would happen if I'm not here. I think every mom probably does that to a certain extent. Maybe not, but I do. I find myself looking at my kids at night when I'm putting them to bed or we're saying prayers, or they're reading to me or something, I'm just looking at them closely, and I examine their whole face for all its perfection. They just look like cherubs to me. And I'm sure in a couple years they won't talk to me and I won't feel that way. I find myself sitting there and looking at them, not saying anything and just being in the moment and thinking, wow, I am so lucky.

Reviewing her precious mom moments brings Gretchen back to that "have-it-all" syndrome. She views those three little words as an obstacle to enjoying the simple pleasures of being a mom. "I think it's just so frustrating for women, and it puts us in this guilt mode that we're supposed to feel like we're these wonder women, and it's just not realistic. It's not. So, I don't feel any guilt—I don't."

But I point out that chronic guilt is a big problem for millions of women. Moms constantly battle feelings of "not being enough," especially when they compare themselves to their peers. Gretchen interrupts me. "Nope. Things just have to fall off of your schedule, so you can do everything that's actually more important. So, let's get rid of the guilt." That little phrase, "get rid of the guilt," just might be Gretchen's mantra for moms. "I just encourage them not to feel guilt in any shape or form, as long as they are an instrumental part of their child's life."

Chronic guilt is a big problem for millions of women.

Gretchen admits she felt relief when she found out that her daughter was okay with her working outside the home as a busy news anchor. "What's really interesting is, my kids are finally getting to the age—especially my daughter who's twelve—where she used to not like the fact that I worked, and now she's like, 'Mom, in Current Events class, I know more than anyone else. You should feel good about that, because it's because of you.' And I'm like, wow, she finally likes me working. It's a good thing."

The economic reality is many moms feel they have to work outside the home even though research suggests that a majority of moms would rather be at home, full-time or part-time, to raise their kids. Gretchen readily admits she stands in the other camp—wanting to work outside the home. She says it's not because she thinks it's better for every mom, but because it's better for her. "I always say that

I'm a better mom because I do work. I feel like I go and do my thing and get fulfilled in whatever way, and then, when I come home, I'm really in the moment with my kids. And I think that, if I wasn't doing that, I maybe wouldn't value my time with them as much as I do now."

No matter how comfortable Gretchen feels with her working mom role, she's aware that a battle rages over which ways of mothering are best. "Mommy wars" cause millions of women to feel contention over a variety of mothering choices: stay at home vs. work outside the home, homeschool vs. public school, breastfeed vs. bottle feed, vaccinate vs. not vaccinate, spanking vs. not spanking, disposable vs. cloth diapers—all conflicts that work to divide rather than unite us as moms. In a survey by Parenting.com, a full 97% of parents admitted to being critical of other people's parenting. Ironically, the same survey noted that 70% said moms today are too defensive about their parenting choices.

Gretchen is all too familiar with the issues used to divide women. She experienced a particularly venomous example after she won the Miss America pageant. At 5 feet, 3 inches and 108 pounds, Gretchen was dubbed "Miss Piggy." She recalls that some of the worst harassment came from women:

> When that happened right after the Miss America Pageant, and one of my judges wrote that entire book, degrading me, calling me "Miss Piggy" and saying I was too fat to win at 108 pounds—I'll never be 108 pounds again! Then the first press conference that I had in New York City, where the female reporter deliberately took me down, asking if I'd ever had sex and if I had ever done drugs. She wanted to

make me look stupid. And that wasn't the way I was raised. So, I remember calling my dad, because everyone loves my father. I said, "Dad, why do people just want to hate me just because? How do I get past this?" He gave me the best advice, and it's so simple… He said, "Gretchen, no matter how hard you try, you are never [going] to get everyone to like you. So, those that you think you can turn around, you invest time in. And those that you think you have no hope with, you walk away." I have faced that almost every single day in my career in television.

That career in television is something Gretchen and I have in common. The two of us first crossed paths in the late nineties, when we both worked for TV stations in Cleveland, Ohio. Gretchen stood out to me back then because she was part of a groundbreaking, two-female anchor team. There was continual scrutiny of their dual performance, perhaps to determine if two women could "cut it" as co-anchors on a newscast.

Gretchen said that kind of skepticism has followed her everywhere. "Every new job I would go to, it became apparent to me that the word on the street was, 'Oh, great. We hired a former Miss America. Here comes a bimbo.' Over time, I learned that I would have to work triple hard to dispel those notions."

Gretchen has labored diligently to dispel numerous negative notions and labels over the years. "The chubby kid" was one of the first labels she overcame, but now she's paying that process forward by offering support to parents whose kids struggle with their own image issues. She believes it's the parents' unique responsibility to build their children up when the world tears them down:

We need to turn back to instilling confidence in our kids through their interior and through their soul, especially with social media now, and kids being denigrated. We've got to go back to inspiring kids to feel good about themselves from the inside and not worry so much about their exterior. Moms used to come up to me after I won Miss America, and they'd say, "How can I help my child to win Miss America?" I would say, "Well, do not do beauty pageants. You know, if she's 5 or 6 or 10 or 12 or 14, my goodness, let's work on who she is as a person from the inside. Let's have her excel in school, let's have her do sports, have her practice her piano or whatever it is. Because when kids put time into something, they get better at it, and they feel better about themselves from the inside. That's how you build self-esteem—not about how you look, not about what tennis shoes you have on, or the jeans, or anything like that. Not if you're fat or thin or black or white, none of that. It's all about building people from the inside out.

I know a few moms may be thinking, it's easy for Gretchen to say we should just work on the "inside" stuff, because she's got it made inside AND out. She's a former Miss America, for goodness' sake! But Gretchen is quick to push past those images and look back to the history that shaped her:

> The most important thing to me is that I have stayed true to who I was growing up in my small town in Minnesota. I love the fact that that's where I grew up and was given such amazing values and had such a great family. No matter what else has happened to me in my life, I will always be the chubby little girl from Anoka, Minnesota, who happened to play a

pretty darn good violin and unexpectedly became Miss America and, more importantly, developed a career and appears on national TV.

If I have done some of the things that I have done in my life and I was able to do it, then I know that I can inspire other people to do the same thing. You know, my life has been a tremendous amount of hard work, but it's also been the American dream, and this is what I do not want to go away in our society for our kids and for our young people. America is about hard work, making the most of our lives, making the most of our families and reaching for the brass ring. Isn't that what we all want?

Gretchen's right. Deep down, most people dream of reaching some kind of "brass ring." She believes moms reading her story can find the inspiration to pursue their own brass rings, if they're willing to work hard. I would add one thought to Gretchen's belief in the potential of every mom. I want moms to see the brass rings of motherhood. I want each mom to tap into her unique ability to mother—to care for her children.

This unique maternal care often extends beyond a mom's own children to caring for the rest of the world. More than their own status, moms often seek their brass rings by contributing to something beyond themselves, not just to their children, but to their family, their town, their nation and their world.

Gretchen also has a desire to contribute to something beyond herself. Her desire came from a somewhat unlikely place—the shame-filled circumstances of sexual harassment. She recalls the demeaning sexual advances she suffered from her boss at FOX News. The incidents prompted her to become a pioneer in the fight against sexual harassment in the workplace. She was an early voice in the wilderness, boldly vocalizing her personal victimization, long before the "MeToo" hashtag became popular. [#MeToo is the well-known social media label representing an international movement against sexual harassment and assault in the workplace.]

You could say Gretchen launched a media tidal wave of sexual harassment claims after she went public with allegations of sexual harassment against her boss at FOX, Roger Ailes. Her lawsuit against Ailes led to a 21st Century Fox internal investigation, during which more than a dozen women came forward with similar harassment claims. Ailes was eventually fired, and Carlson received a settlement and a public apology from 21st Century Fox.

Gretchen ended up leaving her FOX News job, but immediately became a self-appointed warrior for women who have endured sexual harassment. She puts her efforts into helping the women who don't have the kind of standing she does to successfully pursue their own cases.

For starters, she applied her journalistic tenacity to uncovering the silenced cases of women who were demoted, fired or blacklisted after reporting sexual harassment (featured in her Lifetime TV documentary, *"Gretchen Carlson: Breaking the Silence"*). Hollywood also translated Gretchen's story—and her fight—into film. The result was two high-profile projects about her sexual harassment revelations: the major motion picture, "Bombshell," and Showtime's docudrama, "The Loudest Voice."

Ironically, Gretchen's voice has been silenced when it comes to discussing these Hollywood portrayals. She politely told me that she couldn't comment on the films, due to her settlement agreement; however, her silence didn't extend to social media. Gretchen was able to voice her gratitude for the Showtime series on Twitter:

> "This is what women helping women is all about. Thank you, Naomi Watts, for telling a story that honors so many 1000's of women who have also said #metoo. We will continue to speak up and be heard to make the workplace fairer for all. And above all always #befierce #theloudestvoice"

Tweets in response were both positive and negative, but many applauded Gretchen's bravery:

> "... after watching The Loudest Voice... I think we should all celebrate @GretchenCarlson again. And again."

> "You ended his reign of abuse against women who just want to excel at their career. Bravo!!!!"

> "... I thought, it was a show about Roger Ailes, but it was about a HERO, Gretchen Carlson. Woman after woman... sexually abused, by Roger Ailes."

Some social media trolls took a nastier tone toward Gretchen:

> "This series makes clear G Carlson, destroyed conservative TV"

> "She should have resigned. She stayed for the position, and the money."

Critical comments have not stopped Gretchen before, and they're certainly not going to silence her now. She even brought her battle to the halls of Congress, joining a bipartisan coalition of legislators to introduce the "Ending Forced Arbitration of Sexual Harassment Act."

Gretchen's gritty determination to defend women's dignity took the stage in another arena when she agreed to be the chairwoman of the Miss America board of directors. Gretchen almost immediately initiated some of her signature pushback when it came to the pageant. In cooperation with the organization's board, Gretchen enacted some controversial changes. The biggest change? They dropped the iconic swimsuit competition, which created BIG media buzz.

I interviewed Gretchen about that buzz on ChannelMom Radio. Because she went through the swimsuit competition herself thirty years earlier, Gretchen spoke from personal experience. "I don't think women should have to strut around in a bikini and high heels to earn scholarship dollars [from the Miss America Pageant] to go to college."

She rounded out her argument like this: "Miss America has always been emblematic of where women are in society at a particular time. So, this is what we feel is right—to be more inclusive, so that your daughter and my daughter and anyone else who's listening, their daughters, who maybe aren't a size 0, but they're smart and talented, and they want to be a leader of tomorrow and have social impacts on particular issues that are important to them—to all those women we say, 'Here's money for you to go to college.' So that's the mission."

There have been virulent objections to removing the swimsuit strut by those who claim the pageant will be boring without a bathing suit segment. Gretchen points out that the swimsuit competition was only about four-and-a-half minutes of a two-hour broadcast. And she pushes through one final point on behalf of young girls across America. Gretchen doesn't want our young female population to think their bodies are the only thing that make them interesting. "Should we tell our young girls and our daughters that, because we want to know more about you and the substance of you, that's boring?"

As Gretchen seeks to inspire girls and women to be all they can be, I ask what inspires *her*. Without hesitation, she points to her spiritual heritage. Gretchen's grandfather was a minister. She grew up going to Sunday School and now teaches Sunday School alongside her husband Casey. She's been known to defend her faith in the secular arena of TV news; and it's a banner she carries without apology. "My grandfather was a rock star to me. It was like, wow, when I go to church on Sunday, that guy in the pulpit, he's my grandpa. Everyone in town knew who he was, so it was something that I was proud of."

Being proud that her grandpa was a preacher seemed pretty natural to Gretchen, so she suffered a rude awakening when she faced public rejection of the Christian ideals her grandpa stood for:

> When I went on Fox & Friends, which was an ad-lib morning show, we often discussed issues about Christianity, and the one that I detailed in my book was about that ridiculous holiday, Festivus, that was made up on Seinfeld's show. I've got a great sense of humor, I'm all for funny things, but people were actually petitioning state governments to be able to put up a Festivus pole around Christmas time, next to the Nativity scene, and at that point I just went

ballistic. That day was the day that everything changed for me. I said, "This is absolutely deplorable. How dare we make fun of Jesus Christ by putting up a fake religious pole, just because people can." I'm all for democracy, but that just seemed absolutely ridiculous to me. That was the first day that I really, really, really, really started getting attacked in the blogs.

I also got written up in articles where people supported me [basically saying], "Gretchen Carlson is right. We should be talking more about our religious freedoms, and we should be protecting religions that have been in existence forever and ever. We shouldn't give credence to fake religions." And I have to tell you, Jenny, what happened after that was that the number one [thing] people would say to me on the street corner, or when I went home to Minnesota or wherever, was, "Thank you so much for standing up for your Christianity and your values on national TV." It's the number one applause line when I go and give a speech now.

Clearly, Gretchen is respected in some quarters for standing up for what she believes in, and this brings me to what might be my favorite part of Gretchen's story. Gretchen interrupts me to tell me one more thing. Like a typical proud mama, she wants to share a particular highlight in her young daughter's life:

Oh, one other quick thing before I go. I do want to tell you that the second most emotional parenting thing just happened to me over the weekend. My twelve-year-old daughter went to a church retreat that she was very nervous about. And, you know, I've taught Sunday School with my husband for all these years, and I thought, oh, I'm making a difference in my kids' lives, and I'm sure I have in other kids' lives who attend. But, you know, she texted me Saturday night after being at this retreat and hearing the speaker. And she said, "Mom, I just want to let you know that this has been a life-changing experience, and I've decided to give my life to the Lord."

I was at a wedding with my husband, and I showed him the text and I said "Wow." I mean, I guess she's getting older, and she's going to go through confirmation next year in eighth grade. But it was so amazing to see this text and to know that the way in which we raised her and the way in which my family surrounded her with love and Christianity, that she finally understood what it meant. I can't think of anything that made me more proud as a parent.

She adds, "I was overwhelmed. I copied the text and I sent it to my parents and I said, 'Thank you for doing something right with me, so that I could pass that along to her.'"

And that's the last bit of proof from this mom with a famous face that parenting can make all the difference, no matter who you are.

Gretchen's Amazing Mom Secret:
Give yourself a break, because no woman can have it all.

Why **You** Are Amazing #5:
(re-read often)

You do so much as a mom. You are teacher, nurse, chef, chauffeur, cheerleader, maid, counselor, playmate, party planner, professional shopper, artist, wardrobe consultant, pastor and giver of endless hugs and kisses. You are enough. You don't have to try to be everything.

CHAPTER 6
Facing the Fear
Michele Cushatt

Michelle has had cancer. Three times. People are drawn to her life story because of what she's overcome. There's actually something "train wreckish" about Michele's story. You just have to stop and stare. Or listen to her halting speech—evidence of what she's gone through. If you want to be assured that worst case scenarios can build your faith and grow your family, listen to Michele's story.

****

Michele Cushatt's story began with a dream. When she was little, she had a fairytale dream of a future family. But her idyllic vision got interrupted by real life:

> I remember, as a girl, I wanted more than anything to be a mom. I remember imagining it. I didn't play with dolls necessarily but I remember spending time playing and imagining what it would be like to be a mom. This was on my radar for as long as I can remember. In my mind, I was going to be a mom with a bunch of children. I always pictured I'd have about four. Of course, in our imagination, it's very idyllic and perfect.
>
> When I was twenty-one, I got married. A couple years after that, I had my first child. Within months of when he was born, my marriage fell apart and I ended up becoming a single mom. So, that fast, I went from having this kind of picture of what motherhood would look like to having all of that completely shattered, because there was no way to recover the dream of traditional family and motherhood once you're divorced. I mean, you can't go back and make it whole again.

Michele finds common ground with other moms who have suffered the pain of divorce. She knows single motherhood. She understands single moms. Her story is a way of telling their stories. She shares the unique pain and shame that come from being divorced—how it can make a mom feel like she's failed or like she's being judged.

Michele admits the helplessness she felt the day her marriage dream died. "In that relationship, I was a stay-at-home mom. My spouse worked full-time, and I never dreamed that I would end up divorced. Some choices were being made that I didn't have control over. I felt myself in a position where I was basically being delivered a life I never asked for. And what do you do with all of that?"

That question can be even more daunting for a woman of faith. "Because I was a person of faith and very involved in my church community, I found myself being judged pretty frequently for my divorce status. This was back in the nineties when, in the church, the most controversial topic was divorce. I mean in the nineties we didn't have some of the things that we're dealing with today. Those who got divorced, that was kind of like the worst thing you could possibly do."

People may have judged Michele for doing "the worst thing," even if she had little choice in the matter. In reality, she never saw her divorce coming. It wasn't something she wanted. She admits that she yearned to defend herself to those who would judge her, but she also felt a pang of culpability.

"There is this kind of assumption that, if a marriage falls apart, you must not have been able to do something to save it. You still feel some culpability. Even though somebody was making choices that I didn't agree with, I still was somehow not enough of a woman to save the relationship. In my mind, that was a failure on my part."

She thinks that humiliating feelings of failure may impact women especially. "I think we as women think, if we are smart enough and pretty enough and strong enough and talented enough and good enough that we will be able to keep all of our relationships whole, whether it's marriage or parenting. We think that if we can do it all right that everybody's going to be okay. For a long time, I felt like, if I saw a flaw in my marriage or a flaw in my child, that was a direct fallout from my lacking because, if I was good enough, everybody would turn out okay."

That nagging idea of not being "good enough" is a common syndrome for moms. In fact, the CEO of MOPS (Mothers of Preschoolers) International, Mandy Arioto, says it's a common story of moms involved in her organization. Arioto tells me that when she speaks to moms across the nation, they admit they're hounded by feeling that they're "not enough." Her tale echoes Michele's and offers proof that modern moms carry a daunting feeling of inadequacy:

> *That nagging idea of not being "good enough" is a common syndrome for moms.*

> If you look at my book [*Not Enough*], that's the whole thing. Do you wonder if you're enough? This is an ongoing theme in my own life. In marriage, I wasn't enough, because my husband left. In parenting, I wasn't enough, because my kids struggled. In career I wasn't enough, because things didn't always go the way I planned. In health and wellness, I wasn't enough, because I ended up getting sick and getting cancer.

> Obviously, in my mind, these things wouldn't have happened if I would have been enough. We put so much pressure on our own shoulders to make life go according to plan and then, when it doesn't happen,

who are we to blame but ourselves, and that's a whole lot of pressure.

Michele explains how that pressure erupted after the sudden end of her marriage, not long after the birth of her first child. She was a single mom in her twenties, doing her best to take care of her baby boy. "I had a degree in nursing. I couldn't go back to nursing because I couldn't work night shifts and take care of a baby, so I had to completely reinvent myself. Not only did I become a single mom, trying to figure out how to work full-time and pay for a home and a child and all of that, but then, trying to figure out where I fit in the church world was a whole other challenge."

Challenge sometimes came in the form of labels. "Because I became this very flawed woman who couldn't hide the fact, divorce became like a label I carried around that I couldn't hide. Single motherhood became a label I carried around that I couldn't hide. That put me in a position of feeling like I needed to work harder to make up for the many ways that I had failed. I became that overachieving mom that was trying so hard to create a perfect life for her son, because I felt like I had failed him in the worst possible way."

As Michele admits her struggle with outside perceptions, I wonder about her "inside" life. How did she feel about her mom role, now that her picture-perfect vision of a happy home was taken away? Did she work so hard to get ahead of failure that she didn't have time for special moments with her baby? Did she miss out on enjoying the love a mother has for her child?

Michele says she didn't have the luxury of those moments, "because single motherhood is all about working your tail off every day from morning until night." Her blunt answer exposes the plight and pain of single motherhood.

She says her need to work "from morning until night" caused regret over the things she and her son were missing. "There's all kinds of regrets. Every holiday that came around I saw all the other perfectly traditional families, and I was a single mom with a child, negotiating parenting schedules and trying to figure out how to do all of that."

Hers is the modern mothering story of "busy." I ask if it was her "busyness" that led to regrets (as it does for many women). "Well, at that time, I didn't have a choice. It was a matter of working and child care. I mean, what do you do? You have to pay the bills. You don't necessarily enjoy that you have to be that busy, but you have to provide. When you're a single mom you're in survival mode most days, just trying to pay the bills and make sure everybody's fed and make sure you show up and do what you're supposed to do and all of that."

I ask, hopefully, if she had any memorable mothering moments from those days:

> We did have some. We were broke! We had zero money. We couldn't go out to eat. I remember that taking him out for an ice cream cone was like a huge splurge, because we just never could afford to do that.
>
> What we would do was, in the evenings after work and picking him up from daycare, we would sometimes sit on the couch. He was two, three, four years old at the time. And [we'd] watch a funny TV show, or just sit in the same big chair and cuddle and laugh and just have fun, and it would last for maybe

a half an hour. Looking back on that time, from what he can remember and what I remember, those were the precious moments and they were very, very ordinary, nothing spectacular.

The lack of anything spectacular—along with the lack of money—led Michele to a plan of action, a plan she describes with her sardonic sense of humor:

> Out of this pressure to try to make up for what my son was lacking, I decided it would be such a great idea to get remarried. If I had lost the traditional family, I would recreate the traditional family by remarrying. I met this wonderful man at church who had himself been divorced and had two young sons, and so it looked perfect, right? Take a man who was a single dad with two boys and a woman, a single mom with one boy, and they both love God, let's just throw them together in a family and it's all going to work out perfectly.

Michele throws her head back to laugh and says, "for a while." She goes on, "There were many blessings that came from that, but, boy, it was hard. And it was ugly in many ways, because you can't take five people who have come from so much loss and brokenness and throw them in one house and expect everybody to get along. It just doesn't happen. Marriage is hard. Parenting is hard. But, then, when you have marriage and parenting with blended family and stepfamily dynamics, and ex-spouses, and parenting schedules all in one house—man, it gets complicated very fast."

Complicated family dynamics came partly from the
competition between their three sons. Eventually, one of
those sons chose to live with a relative and, just months
later, Michele and her husband asked another son with
behavioral issues to leave their home:

> As we went through the teenage years, we had boys
> that made decisions that we didn't agree with. Now, I
> should add here, in many traditional families they
> have teenagers that make decisions they shouldn't
> make, and they have children who decide to go spend
> a week or two at a friend's house rather than come
> home, because they don't like the rules. Or they have
> a child that they have to ask to leave once they
> become an adult because of choices they've made.

> Those aren't necessarily unique to us, but the
> blended family dynamic, the stepfamily dynamic,
> added an extra level of complication on top of that.
> There's not the cohesiveness and the bondedness
> that is often present in the traditional family to help
> carry you through that.

At least 16 percent of American children live in a blended
family in some form, and Michele touches on an issue that
many blended families struggle with. "We had less time to
bond as a family. We became a family when the boys were
four, seven, and nine. They had already gone through a big
chunk of their life without us being a tight family unit.
When you go into that adolescent phase, where all the
hormones and all the emotions get turned upside down
anyway, and then you have that added complication of this

stepfamily dynamic, it just makes it extra difficult for everyone."

Michele admits to a kind of pressure that's common for mothers in blended families and stepfamilies. "Navigating that phase of motherhood with a blended family, if I didn't feel a failure as a mom before, I definitely felt like a failure then. What does this say about my motherhood if I have a child who would rather not live here? What does this say about my value as a mom when I have children that would much rather do the exact opposite of what I want them to do? Being that motherhood was the most important thing in my life outside my faith and my marriage, that caused a massive identity crisis."

I tell her I'm struck by how she insists on holding tight to the value of motherhood, despite the enormous pain it's causing her. She laughs at the thought of clinging, white-knuckled, to her mom role. "Yeah, I loved motherhood kind of like I love running a marathon, even though every ounce of my body hurts. I still love it. I still loved my boys, but, boy, it's painful. I think that's what I did not know going into motherhood, how painful it truly can be. And I'm not just talking, oh, boohoo. I miss them when they're gone. I mean, feeling like your heart is being completely wrenched because you love them so much, and yet you start to realize how little control you truly have."

The lack of control became more apparent as Michele's boys grew old enough to make their own decisions. "To sit back and watch your children making decisions that you know will affect them for quite some time and not being able to do anything about it is a horribly painful experience."

She points to that painful paradox of mother love. "They say the more you love, the more pain you experience. If I hadn't loved them, if I hadn't loved motherhood, it would not have been painful for me. But the fact that it was excruciating, especially during those teen years and post-teen years, was a very powerful indicator of how deeply I loved them and how much I was invested in this whole thing called motherhood."

As Michele tells her story of struggle and family turmoil, I think of her sizable home in a well-kept neighborhood, and I'm aware that people driving by might never guess the struggles that went on behind her brightly colored front door. I meander through her spacious rooms and sit next to her baby grand piano. I take in her smiling family photos and mementos from world travels. I think of the temptation I've had to envy her, a successful author, speaker and former host of a popular podcast. I'm struck by the huge contrast between the outward appearance of her life and the inner battle she's had to wage when life has thrown her brutal curve balls.

She begins to talk about her worst days in the batter's box, recounting a series of curve balls that landed with literal body blows. "Yeah, so my oldest son graduated from high school, and my second son was halfway through his senior year when, on Thanksgiving 2010, I got a phone call from a doctor diagnosing me with cancer for the first time. It was a cancer of the tongue, which I didn't know existed. I had never even heard of that possibility and it made no sense. I'm not a smoker. I'm a health person. I love to run, so it didn't make sense for a thirty-nine-year-old mom and wife to get cancer of the tongue. That's something that you would think a seventy-year-old smoker would get, not somebody young and healthy."

She admits that her immediate response was shock and fear. "This completely threw me. Here we are, with one of our children out of high school, another about ready to be done with high school. We're feeling that we're getting close to the light at the end of the tunnel and all of a sudden, I'm in a massive health crisis and we don't know what's going to happen. Talk about another identity crisis! That whole situation makes me do kind of a re-evaluation of my whole life. I mean, you can't go through life and death issues without taking stock."

Michele took stock of her life and found that a lot of it was invested in motherhood and family. "What kind of mom am I? What kind of woman am I? What kind of wife am I? Have I done everything I needed to do? Then I find myself in that position again of thinking I haven't done enough, I need to do more, I need to be a better mom. All of those kinds of things. That fear put me into overdrive in motherhood again."

Staying alive to continue mothering became a primary motivator for Michele as she battled through her cancer diagnosis and treatment. She argued her case to live before God:

> "Come on, God, my kids need me. You wouldn't put them through more loss, so come on. I need you to step up here and fix this!" Over the months that followed, it wasn't so much a physical battle as an emotional battle, to fight against the constant daily fear, which ended up being a theme in my life because I was operating from a place of fear with my health. I was operating from a place of fear with my parenting.
>
> All my mothering was about trying to prevent bad things from happening, and I had been operating

from a place of fear in my career, my marriage, everything else. Fear, I started to discover through this whole cancer journey, had been really the driving force behind my mothering, my parenting, all of it, which is quite convicting.

Ah, fear. I get this battle. Fear has been a driving force in my daily life—my thoughts, my relationships, my career, my mothering. Even my vacations have been carried out with a measure of fear. Over the years, worst case scenarios have played out in my head countless times, allowing fear to rule the day in my life. Michele and I do not live alone in the "Land of Fear." I'm aware that fear is pervasive for many moms. But I also know that most moms would like to be set free from their fears.

Michele reveals that fear was, overall, the worst part of her cancer battle. She had to confront how real her faith was when pitted against her fears. It was a confrontation between Michele and fear, more than between Michele and God. Even though she questioned how she could have developed tongue cancer with her healthy lifestyle, she says she never really questioned God with "Why, God, why?"

I need to decide if I really believe what I say I believe.

Not with cancer. I did with my divorce. I went through the "Why, God, why?" with my whole divorce, because that was so out of left field and not what I had prayed for. In some ways, the whole divorce crisis of faith had prepped me for this later crisis. God had done some real work to establish my faith; I didn't question any more that something bad would happen. I just had to then really wrestle with, if I really believe in God who sent His son Jesus to rescue me and to prepare a place for me, then no matter what happens, it only gets better for me from here. It's one thing to say that. It's another thing to truly believe it and live believing it, having to face the reality that, although I talk about heaven and I talk about my faith and I talk about eternity, it still hasn't planted itself deeply enough in me that a cancer diagnosis didn't cause an incredible amount of fear.

It forced me to face the fact that I need to decide if I really believe what I say I believe. If I really believe what I say I believe, then this fear has no place here. I need to fight against it. So that's where the crisis was. It wasn't that I didn't believe in God. It was more of I need to decide if I'm just a lip Christian or if this is real for me.

Ironically, Michele realized the only cure for her fear was a death scare. "The only way we make peace with that is by facing a life-or-death situation. There's no way for your faith to dig down to those roots until you have to. I mean, it takes a crisis for your faith to actually start digging down into that place of wrestling with your mortality. You can think about it ahead of time, and you can try to prepare ahead of time, but it's one of those lessons that you only learn in the trenches."

The trenches would end up being a familiar residence for Michele. However, it was that first time she stepped below ground, beneath the happy surface of daily life, that she began to find healing for her fear:

After that first diagnosis of cancer, after going through scans and surgery and everything, it turned out to be a best-case scenario. They caught it early and they did a surgery to remove a small section of my tongue. It took a couple weeks to recover. Obviously not fun. Not comfortable. It was hard.

> But in that first bout with cancer, what proved to be the most difficult was the internal change, the fear, because I couldn't un-know this. I couldn't go back to that pre-cancer ignorance where I thought I would live forever. That first diagnosis, as minor as it was, shook me to the core and forced me to face the reality that this life will not last forever. And that was massive.

I think the concept of mortality is "massive" for many moms. It's a constant source of fear, as it hovers in the corners of a mom's mind, reminding her that she will not be on the planet with her children forever. Many moms fear that "final" separation from their children. Just as kids fear separation from their moms:

> What followed in the months after that was a lot of fear, a lot of wrestling, a lot of trying to put my face on the floor and trust God's sovereignty. I'm sorry, but that's not easy. I fought that because I didn't want God's sovereignty. I wanted to live. I just did. I didn't want to leave my kids. I felt like, but my kids need me, my husband needs me, all of that kind of stuff.

> After I moved past the fear, the doctors gave me great news. They caught it early. We put it in a box

and put it on a shelf, because it was done. The doctor said, "We got it all. It's not going to come back. You're fine. It's highly curable." All of that. Over the next couple years, I'd still have my six-month checkups, but it just wasn't part of my daily life anymore.

But her daily life was about to bring her back to the trenches and, this time, the call to battle was the ring of her phone:

> After that first cancer diagnosis—about eight months later—we got a phone call, very random, unexpected, from someone who knew of a mom who could no longer take care of her children. The specifics are not important, but she had some addictions that she struggled with that made it impossible for her to care for her children. These were twin four-year-olds and a five-year-old. This person was coming to my husband and I and asking us, "Will you take them?"

> Let's just say that I did not take that request lightly! I mean, we've had our share of parenting. We knew how hard it was. Here we were almost done parenting, so to go back and start over again was very hard. Yet at the same time, our own journey through the unexpected nature of life, through cancer, had opened our hearts and eyes to people who were also dealing with unexpected life. I mean, what more than three children who are about to lose their mom?

Twenty-four hours later, Michele and Troy went to pick up their three new charges. And, as Michele says, this is when they embarked on a strange "journey to parenting three kids that were not our biological kids and who came from a place of trauma. If we thought the blended family, step-family thing was hard, adding three kids from trauma into that dynamic just multiplied that complication and hardness a hundredfold."

Adding three traumatized little ones to her fold tested Michele's mothering instincts to their core. Many parents have a hard enough time caring for kids they birthed and bonded with through shared DNA. But Michele and Troy agreed to take on children who were strangers with unknown baggage. Suddenly they were responsible for nurturing these not-yet-our-kids through thick and thin.

Personally, when I hear about adoption and fostering stories like Michele's and Linda's (Chapter 4), I am humbled. In fact, I'm amazed by the choice to parent kids that somebody else decided not to parent. It's one of the most sacrificial and selfless acts any adult can commit to.

Michele expands on the depth of the sacrifice. "You have three young people who have gone through unbelievable grief and loss and trauma that you are throwing into a household with a mom, a dad and three other kids that have gone through grief and loss and trauma, and asking them all to be a family. Here we are, eight of us, trying very imperfectly to figure out what family looks like now. That process in the years that followed was just hard."

She admits that another one of her idyllic visions had to die. "All my rules and dreams about mothering were thrown out the window, because they just lost their mom, they just got removed from their mom's house and placed in a house with two other adults, and they had gone through all kinds of trauma. They are four- and five-year-olds who are way too young to know how to verbally process that, so they act out. And here are Troy and I, trying to figure out how to bring some measure of healing and love to them while we're still dealing with our own stuff."

If you're a mom who feels like your family life doesn't measure up, reeks of dysfunction, or is not at all what you dreamed of, take heart. Michele's family dreams were dashed too. She may have had an attractive external life— lovely home, impressive speaking career, attractive appearance—but that couldn't compensate for what was unfolding in her internal world, the behind-closed-doors stuff.

I bring up Michele's childhood dream of being a happy mom with lots of kids. "I know, I got my big family. Just a very odd way to get it," Michele admits. "It's a process, it's a process."

That difficult process was about to be interrupted by an unwelcome discovery.

"Not quite three and a half years later, I found another spot on my tongue that was very, very painful, and I went back to the doctor. They did another biopsy and, sure enough, the cancer was back. I was stunned, the doctor was stunned, my family was stunned. None of us expected this. This time it was more advanced. They scheduled a surgery within a few weeks. They took out one-third of my tongue, which was pretty sizable. Nobody wants to lose one-third of their tongue. It took me about eight weeks to recover from that surgery."

This is when Michele was hit on all fronts. Everything in her life was exposed to this latest bout with cancer—her family, her mothering, her marriage, her appearance, and, because the cancer involved Michele's tongue, her speaking career:

My whole career, my way of earning income, is really speaking. Writing doesn't earn very much money, so speaking is the way that I pay my bills. To have the very instrument of our livelihood [her tongue]—now a third of it is gone—was significant. Now we have a whole different kind of fear. What if I can't do what I feel made to do? You know, you have someone who is made to run marathons and you cut off their legs. How do you reconcile that?

For me, that's what it felt like. How will I do what I love doing more than anything else if I can't talk? I slowly started to speak again, to learn how to eat again. I did my first speaking engagement eight weeks after that surgery, which was just amazing! And, ironically enough, at that first speaking engagement, I get a phone call from my father, and he had just been told he was terminal with pancreatic cancer. Here I am, just closing the door on my cancer journey, celebrating that I can still speak, and I get a phone call from my dad while I'm in the hotel, telling me that he has somewhere between ten months and two years to live.

Michele's life in the trenches continued. Cancer not only cut into her tongue, but the scourge of cancer now threatened her heart, as she faced the loss of her dad. "He lived three months. August 19th, 2014, he died, and, I mean, it was really less than four or five months after my second diagnosis. So fast. Then here we are. At this point, I've had cancer twice, my dad's had cancer, we've gone through all kinds of divorce and stepfamily and everything, and I'm like, okay, I've had my share. Surely God won't give me anymore. It's enough."

Sometimes our version of enough is just not big enough. And Michele learned this lesson the hard way:

About two months after I buried my dad, the doctor called again. Cancer was back for the third time. This time it came back so aggressively, so fast, they scheduled surgery within just a couple weeks. That surgery was nine hours long. They took out two-thirds of my tongue. They took out tissue and blood vessels from my arm, wrist to elbow, to rebuild my tongue. Took out an area of my leg about the size of an iPhone 6 Plus to rebuild my arm. Cut my neck twice, about six to eight inches, taking out blood vessels and lymph nodes to rebuild all of these different parts of my body. They put in a feeding tube that I would get all my nourishment from for about five or six months. They put in a tracheotomy for six weeks to help me breathe and not choke from everything that was happening.

Then, after giving me about four weeks to recover from that, they started intense chemotherapy and radiation. They did radiation every day for six weeks, and after that they put me in the hospital again, where they did what's called Braki therapy, where they inject radiation directly into my mouth. I'll spare you the details, but you can imagine what that would entail. By the time all was said and done I had incisions and scars on my leg, my arms, my neck and my mouth. I had my feeding tube, my tracheotomy, and I had burns from my chest to my nose.

Almost too horrifying to imagine, I find myself nearly nauseous as Michele retells the story. And I'm overwhelmed by the fact that Michele was still trying to be a mom in the midst of this unimaginable, personal agony. "I was on 24/7 narcotics. We're talking not your Percocet. We are talking massive Fentanyl and liquid morphine, just to take the edge off. I lost like thirty-five pounds. I could not get off the couch. Trying to be a mom and wife.... I was throwing up multiple times a day every day for six months, with a feeding tube, with everything rebuilt, with burns everywhere. You can just imagine what that would entail."

I imagine it's like hell on earth, and she agrees:

> I had never known a human being could suffer like that. I did not know it was even possible. I remember thinking, before all this happened, when I would hear about people who wished to die, where their experience in life was so painful that they actually wished to die, and I couldn't understand that.
>
> I understand that now. I understand how a human being can be experiencing such incredible pain, physical pain and suffering twenty-four hours a day for months, where it can get you to a place where you are utterly despairing of life. When I hear somebody that's at that place now, I have no judgment for them. Zero. There is a kind of physical suffering that most of us have no clue about. And now I know.

When I ask if she wished to die during that time, Michele says matter of factly, "I begged to die. I would pray. My greatest fear was that I would live. Isn't that interesting?"

Get out the checkered flag and wave it. This desperate time marked the official end to Michele's fear of death. "Yeah, I'm not afraid to die anymore. I still have some lingering apprehension about pain and suffering, because I know how bad it can be. I would never want to go back and experience that pain and suffering again. To stay alive in that place of physical pain is a worse thing than death."

Death was no longer a fearsome image for Michele. Her faith in God and Heaven had been purified in the fiery furnace of her trials. She'd become convinced, again, that when she dies, she will see God and experience heaven. Michele's fear of death was gone. "I just remember so many days, I'm like, 'God, please just let me go. Don't make me live through this pain anymore,' which sounds so crazy, but those who have experienced intense physical suffering know exactly what I'm talking about."

This is where we see the story of Michele Cushatt intersect with the story of Kara Tippetts (Chapter 8). It's an intersection of shared circumstances: two moms facing cancer, two moms leaning on the hope of their faith against all odds, and, two moms who decide that suffering is worth it. They accept suffering for the teacher it is. For the humility it engenders. For the love it grows. And for the sweet glimpses of unimaginable grace it ushers in:

> The volume of lessons, the richness that God granted through this is almost beyond words. It's almost impossible for me to sum up. It's impossible for me to sum up the glory that God allowed me to get a glimpse of through all of this. Again, I would never go back. I would never want to go back and experience this again, so I say this very soberly. I don't want to say it and try to put a red bow on it. It's

horrible, horrible, horrible. And there are still moments when I think back on those times that I feel the trauma from it just revisit me. I still have moments of crying and grief over it.

It was trauma. There's no other way to say it. And yet, at the same time, the reality of God's presence and His goodness and His purposes. He allowed me to see just a glimpse of that, and it re-oriented my faith, re-established my faith in a way that couldn't have been accomplished in any other way.

I am humbled by Michele's brave acceptance of grace found in suffering. Through tears, I tell Michele she has changed my life by tenderly revealing that she's honored to have suffered. She explains that her suffering drew her closer to the God who chose to suffer for us. It helped her come to know Him and trust Him through shared suffering:

That became so rich to me, and it set apart every other claim to faith. Everything else. Because that's truly what I needed. In that moment I realized, when we're healthy and strong and life is going well, we don't think much about the cross. We don't need it so much. But a time is coming for every single one of us when we are going to be face on the floor in some kind of pain—whether physical or emotional—it's coming. It's just part of the human condition.

And when that happens, we don't need our intellect, good retirement accounts, happy Christmas gatherings with our families, big cars and nice houses. We need a savior that suffered. And when I was lying on the couch in so much pain, I remember thinking how silly all of the ways I'd spent my life were, worrying about what kind of car to buy, or worrying about our retirement, or worrying about what kind of grades my kids got in school. All of this seemed so completely silly in the light of our mortality. In that moment, all that mattered to me is that there was a God and that He loved me enough to endure unbelievable pain to make sure that I would have an eternity free of pain. That meant everything to me... it's everything.

I'm aware that not everyone sees the "everything" Michele sees. Not every mom shares her faith. I have sympathy for this faithless position. I haven't always believed what Michele believes, so I can identify with the mom who has big doubts. And my heart goes out to the mom who doesn't see God in the universe. That's why I've felt compelled to share how Michele's doubts and fears were slain by a virtual trip to hell and back. I ask Michele to consider the skeptical mom when she talks about her restored faith that God is real. She struggles for the right words.

"How do you sum that up in just a few thoughts? This is all I can say. I found myself during those months and months and months and months. It's been two years now, and it's really only been in the last five, six months that I've felt more myself. This healing process has been a good, solid year and a half to two years."

She continues to unwrap an answer to my question with her quintessential honesty. "During those long months of suffering and pain, I found myself wanting to crawl up to the cross more and more. As Christians, we spend a lot of time celebrating Easter. The tomb is empty. Jesus has risen. This whole idea of a resurrected savior is huge for the Christian faith. We want to believe that God lives. But what I found is that it was so critical to me, so important to me, not that Jesus rose from the dead, but that He suffered. And the fact that, in all the different faiths and religions and claims, nothing else claims to have a deliverer that's willing to suffer for us."

The suffering servant, sent to save struggling humans, is what has been most convincing to Michele:

> By definition, God is perfect and holy and glorious and set apart and removed and all this. For Him to exit perfection—a place where there is zero pain, zero suffering, zero tears, zero grief—and come to earth to go through unbelievable agony. He said He did it because "You are precious and honored in my sight and because I love you." That makes no sense to me. In those moments when I was suffering, and I was suffering to a lesser extent, the fact that God would abandon perfection because of His affection for me and experience that kind of grueling pain.

> I kept thinking about Jesus in the garden, when Jesus would say as He was praying, "God, please, if there be any way, take this cup from me." It sounded a lot like my prayers: "God, please, please, just let me die. Don't make me do this." And yet, at the end of every one of Jesus' requests to God, He would say, "Not my will, but yours." He so trusted in the purposes and affection of God that He would willingly subject Himself to that kind of horrible pain and suffering.

"It was worse than yours," I say quietly.

"Worse than mine. Worse than mine," she admits.

This brings us to Michele's hard-fought mothering secret, a secret molded in the womb of suffering. Nurtured in the daily gift of grace. And birthed at the fruition of her unfaltering faith.

Michele's perspective sheds light on the true importance of motherhood, which is missed in the hustle and bustle of our culture. I ask her what motherhood means to her now. What is the secret she's discovered that a busy, distracted society might have missed?

"I think, as an American culture, as a Western culture, we have put such a high price tag on our comfort in life, on-going through life and having life be exactly the way we want it to be, that we avoid anything that challenges us, that is difficult, that's hard, that makes us uncomfortable, even to the point of motherhood. Many of us would avoid motherhood because we think, what if we make a mistake or what if it's hard or whatever. We work so hard to minimize any kind of pain and discomfort."

She's right. Western culture puts a premium on avoiding discomfort. Seat heaters. Pain killers. Microwaves and riding lawn mowers. Michele observes, "First of all, that's a faulty premise. It's not possible to avoid everything uncomfortable. And,

> *Motherhood, more than anything else, is about discipleship.*

second, it's those things that are the most grueling, those things that require strength and sweat and tears, that actually develop us. If we're constantly avoiding those things that are hard, we're not just shortchanging the world, we're actually shortchanging ourselves."

She reveals, specifically, how this applies to motherhood.

Motherhood has become one of the best places for me to understand the selfless love of God, for me to face how far I am from that. If I would boil down motherhood into the single, most important thing, twenty, thirty years ago, I would've said that motherhood was all about baking cookies together, and creating nice memories around the birthdays and holidays, and making sure we did family vacations, and that we played games together, and created neat moments together, and created almost this Hallmark picture of family, right? That was what motherhood is.

No, I think motherhood, more than anything else, is about discipleship. It's about telling your children about the Jesus who loves them and came for them. That's really what matters. I almost feel like that sounds so trite. It's not. We put so much pressure on motherhood, with all these other things, the Valentine's boxes that we help our kids create for the party at school and the Halloween costumes that we feel like we need to sew or go out and buy. Boy, we work so hard to create these fun memories for our kids. And the truth is, even though those are nice moments, if we haven't taught our children how to deal with pain and suffering, what they're going to do in those moments when their life doesn't go according to plan, if we haven't helped them learn how to build their life on that foundation of faith, then it doesn't matter how many crafts we do and [how many] cookies we bake.

"How good our Facebook pictures are," I interject. And she answers, almost like a preacher from a pulpit, "The scrapbooks don't matter if our kids don't know that there is a God who has a plan for them, who will not fail them no matter what. That's it. That's what motherhood is about. All the other things, cheat all the other things. Be the worst mom in school who never does a Valentine's box for your kids, but make sure your kids know there is a real God, that His word can be trusted and that He is their anchor. Nothing else. You get that right and you've succeeded as a mom."

This is where she humbly admits, "That's what I missed. I worked so hard to create a perfect picture of motherhood that I missed that motherhood is simply about discipleship with your babies—teaching them about the love of God."

Michele's Amazing Mom Secret:

Disciple your babies. Teach them about the love of God.

Why **You** Are Amazing #6:
(re-read often)

As a mom, you work to bring your kids joy even when you don't have joy. Although it's one of the hardest things for a human to do, you choose sacrificial love. Putting your child's wellbeing before your own. Even when you're hurting, you want your kids to be happy. Your mothering has the unique power to exhibit God's sacrificial love to your kids. Is there anything greater?

CHAPTER 7
Overcoming A Childhood Nightmare
Mari Burelle

"If you could see the things I see, hidden deep inside of you. There's strength, there's fight, there's hope, and life. Let it all shine through."

From "Stand Up,"
Lyrics by Mari Burelle

Some nights, when she's singing on stage, she remembers the beatings. The days as a little girl when she thought her mother might kill her. Or destroy her beautiful voice. But today, Mari sings on stages throughout the world. And she sings with a purpose.

✳✳✳✳✳✳

Mari's story is painful to tell because of its brutality. But it's also a story that must be told because of its message. A message of hope. Hope for any mom who has ever feared that she'd be a bad parent because her parents were. It's for every mom who is afraid they won't overcome the wrongs of their childhood. Afraid she'll repeat those same wrongs with her own kids.

Mari Burelle is here with a musical message for moms who don't want to repeat what was done to them. For moms who want to do better for their kids.

Mari is a colorful parade of purple wigs, outrageous outfits and huge personality—like a Mardi Gras celebration announcing her Latin pop diva image. She's completely at home in recording studios, concert venues and media interviews. But her musical life was preceded by something more dissonant. Mari's childhood years were overwhelmed by horrific abuse at the hands of her biological mom.

For as long as she can remember, Mari had a deep fear. She feared that if someone is abused, they will become an abuser. If a girl has a bad mom, she will become a bad mom. Mari imagined a brutal reckoning if she ever had a child of her own—destined to carry on the pattern of abuse modeled by her own mom.

Mari paints a picture of that pattern in shades of black and blue. "I wear wigs for fashion, but when I first got into them it was just to hide that I was ashamed of my cultural hair. My mother hated brushing it because it was thick, kinky, curly hair. She would brush it 'til it bled. She would beat my scalp with the brush and she would tell me how ugly I was. She would hate the hair so much that she would actually tie it to the bunk beds, and she would let me literally just hang there."

That begins Mari's story of unimaginable mistreatment at the hands of her mom. Her mother would hit her, beat her, and call her "fat" and "ugly." She says some friends have asked, "Did you hate her for that?" Her answer: "I really didn't hate her. I was very angry with her for doing those things to me. The thing is, I was always scared of when the next punch was coming, when the next word or abuse was coming. But what I was thinking in my head was, okay, if I take this like a champ, am I gonna get something else later? I was always thinking that, maybe if I allow her to deck me a really good one, then I'll be done for the day. That was my train of thought, and that's not normal, you know?"

Not much seems normal in Mari's childhood. Neglect. Taunts. Threats. Beatings. These things haunted her as a kid. Mari recollects one of her mom's most sinister deeds: her mom once terrorized her with a threat of battery acid, telling Mari that she would dip her hands in it.

If you're wondering how her mom could be so diabolical, she explains that her mother was addicted to drugs, even while carrying Mari in her womb. "I was actually born premature and really small, which is funny, cuz today I'm fun-size, and back then I wasn't [laughs]." Her premature birth would mark the first time—but not the last—that Mari would need hospital care during her young life. She says that her mom's abuse sent her to the hospital several times:

> One of the times, she had told me that the pills that my grandmother had were candy. So, I had a bunch of them, thinking they were candy. For some reason, I don't even remember tasting [them] even to this day, if they had any taste. The next thing I knew, I woke up in the hospital. I think she thought I was like gone or something, but I was still there. I just

remember this black drink that I had to keep drinking to get the charcoal through my body to clean my system, to get all the drugs out of me.

I remember being in the hospital for that, and then another time when she beat me black and blue. This was actually the last time in the hospital, because I finally admitted it [the abuse]. My adopted mother said, "Why didn't you say anything all that time?" It was just because I was scared to say anything. I was threatened: "Your life is gonna be taken. I'm gonna beat you worse."

These tales of abuse are confirmed by the woman who would eventually adopt her. Mari's adoptive mom, Linda, says she'd get calls from the state about the abuse Mari was suffering at the hands of her biological mom, including holding Mari under water in the bathtub and stabbing her repeatedly with a fork.

It was after those reports that Linda stepped in to bring a little light into Mari's dark world. Linda and her husband Gary began providing part-time foster care to Mari and her siblings. Linda recalls the heavy baggage these kids dragged behind them. She explains that Mari would cry out in the middle of the night, and when they'd come into her bedroom to check on her, Mari would be shaking uncontrollably, because she thought her mother was hiding in a tree outside her room. And when her husband would drive Mari and her siblings back to their biological mom's home, Linda says the kids were so terrified, they would soil themselves.

Mari developed an internal lifeline during those years of abuse, by holding onto a dream of something better. "I always knew in my heart that one day I'd be fully out. I'm a big dreamer, and I would always dream of where I wanted to be, and I would pray. I remember saying, one day I'm gonna be with my adopted parents all the time. I'm never gonna have to go through this again. I'm just gonna get through today. It was just living literally day by day, just surviving, and just saying, if I make it through this, if I make it through that punch, if I make it through this hospital visit, I'll finally get there one day."

Until "one day" arrived, Mari was forced to withstand not only physical abuse but verbal abuse as well. "She would tell me that I would not amount to anything and that she'd make sure of it. And I know that doesn't seem like a big deal. The reason that hurt so bad is because I had siblings, but she chose me."

Chosen for abuse. Maybe harsh words and beatings convince their victims they're chosen on purpose for this punishing life. Maybe that's a big reason they don't speak up or run out.

This thought spurs flashbacks in my mind. I flash back to scenes from the award-winning movie, *I, Tonya,* about Olympic skater Tonya Harding. I think of the cruel language and physical violence Tonya was said to have suffered at the hands of her ex-husband and her mother. Yet Tonya returned to them again and again. I'm stunned by how the abused return to their abusers, frequently offering forgiveness and unbendable hope for both themselves and those who abuse them.

Mari shares her own thought process during the years of repeated abuse. "I mean, for me, it wasn't even because she was my mother. You know how a wife will go back with her spouse, even if he's cheated or abused her. People are always thinking they're crazy. I honestly actually felt bad for her [her mother]. I was so wise beyond my years. I had to grow up quickly because of the way I was treated. I honestly felt like it was my duty to stay and take those beatings, cuz I felt like maybe, if she took it out on me, she wouldn't hurt somebody else. I felt that responsibility."

Mari felt so responsible that she thought it might be her duty to hide the abuse from everyone, including her foster parents. "They tried to believe the best, but they obviously know, if you're capable of doing drugs when you have a child inside your womb, that you're not the most stable of characters. So, they knew she had tendencies. Every time that I would come home, they would see that I would hide under the seat of the Suburban, because I didn't want to go in to visit her. I didn't want to have to leave them. And so they would see all those things and I would keep denying it, until that last time."

She says that's the day—after years of being questioned about her biological mom's parenting—that she finally admitted to Linda and Gary just how bad it had been. It was not long after this that Linda and Gary adopted Mari. The adoption, it's safe to say, would save Mari's life.

This makes me think of the other women and men who step in to take responsibility for struggling or abused children that are not theirs by birth. Foster parents. Adoptive parents. Grandparents. And other types of "parents"—teachers, coaches, childcare workers, social workers, neighbors and more. I think of these people as unsung heroes. Heroes that we should recognize.

Mari had two such heroes in her life—specifically, two women who stepped in to mother her. Both her adoptive mom and her mother-in-law saw the mothering void in Mari's life and became the "step-in moms" she needed. As I reflect on these women, I realize that there are millions of step-in moms who accept the challenge that Yvonne Pointer gave us in Chapter 2, to be mothers to more than the children we birthed.

Mari's mom, Linda, accepted that challenge when she chose to mother Mari:

> Oh yeah. She's my rock, my best friend. She's everything to all of us. You would not find a sweeter soul. She's like, "I'm the one. God gave you to me and I'm your mother, and I'm not going to let anyone else take that from me." She just gives and gives of her heart.
>
> She showed me that I was beautiful inside and out. She showed me the true value [of] being a mother, that I didn't have to take on those tendencies that I was taught. Even when I did those things, she disciplined me. She said, "Listen, you're starting to be angry. You said you didn't want to be like this person [her biological mom]," and she would love me enough to tell me, "Don't start to go down that path." Always just patting me on the back. There was also a stern rebuke at times when I needed that!

Linda explains her commitment to mothering like this, "Once we have a child, that's a calling. We're stewards of this young life." And when it comes to fostering and adoption, Linda says, "We can make a difference. We can rescue the ones that need us so badly. We make a decision in our heart to honor God and then He gives us that love for them."

Notably, it was Linda's own difficult childhood (including her parent's broken marriage) that led her to pray that one day she could be an answer to the prayers of broken children. She explains that she wanted to overcome her own parents' past by having a solid marriage and taking in children that needed solid parenting.

We can make a difference. We can rescue the ones that need us so badly.

Linda's adoptive mothering had a huge impact on Mari—specifically on her own future as a mom. Linda gifted Mari with a legacy of good mothering, rescuing her from the poor example set by her biological mom.

"It's funny, cuz, in Spanish, her name means 'beautiful,' and I always tell her she's Linda, the most beautiful person in the world."

Beauty was visible in Linda's selfless approach to being a mom. "She looks at me as her assignment, just like when you go to work and you have something to do for that day, you're going to get it done. She's not going to let me go until the day that she goes home to be with the Lord. She says, 'This is what I know God wants for you.' She is obedient to what God wants to do and not to her own selfish reasons, and I think that's so admirable."

"Assignment" might seem like an impersonal term, but it's also a term of commitment. If a mother saw each of her children as an honorable "assignment," designed specifically for her, wouldn't that make a mom more likely to complete the assignment to the best of her ability?

But just as not all school assignments are easy, the assignment to raise a child is not always easy either. Mari recalls being a difficult assignment for her adoptive parents, despite all they'd done for her.

"I had just finished high school and instead of going to college, I went to sing in the clubs and bars. I started to have a couple cigarettes. I started to drink every night.

I never slept with anybody else. I was always scared, because my mom did raise me up with that. I'd be scared if a guy kissed me, I'd get an STD. I was like, I'm not going to church. I'm going to sign a contract in the world, which I did, with a major label back then. I wasn't ready. I was so miserable. And my spirit felt so scared. I never like to sound religious, but it is so real. I can't even begin to tell you the things that were happening to me. I don't even know how I'm alive."

She gives an example of the "real" world she faced, far removed from the wholesome care of her adoptive family. "One day I was sleeping outside a Checkers in the ghetto in Orlando, and this guy offered me a ride home. For some reason I was so out of it that I got into his car, and he pulled down his pants and tried to make me touch him. I remember being so scared that I jumped out of the car."

It was a "scared straight" moment for Mari that changed everything. The change began when she came across an ad announcing auditions for a church talent show. Mari went to the audition with plans to leave everything related to her secular music life behind. "As soon as I walked through those doors, I felt home and like I need to be here." Mari believed walking into that church was divinely orchestrated. In fact, she says that an elderly man once told her that she'd end up in a church just like the one she walked into. He also predicted she'd find her future husband in that same church, which she did. Mari says she's often leaned on "God promises" like that one:

I was in the projects one day and these two men
came up to me. I was nine years old. They told me
God was going to use my gift, and I was going to sing
all over the world for His glory. He would send
people to tell me what the next step was to take.
And, literally, along the way, I've been told exactly
that, from strangers in the airport to people at
the park.

It's not just like you have to go to church to hear
from God. He's everywhere. He wants to speak to you
everywhere. You don't always have to think along
religious lines. I've gotten the word from somebody
in a bar. That's where He is. He's outside. He's in the
hospital. He's on the battlefield. He's looking for us
when we're broken, when we're messed up, when
we're going the wrong way. That's what people need
to see. That's why I follow Him, cuz, if not, then
we're living in this fake religious world.

The "fake religious world" is something Mari has
experienced personally. She says she witnessed it in the
Christian music industry and in her own church life. She
points to the sort of "churchy" presentations that don't seek
God as much as they seek to glorify human talents. Mari
laments the pressure to impress people more than to love
God. She watched that pressure seep into her own, high-
profile job at her church. As a singer in the worship band,
she watched that position exact its toll on her relationship
with her husband Ivan:

It started to be I was there seven days a week. He'd
wait for me until three o'clock in the morning

sometimes. I never got to see him and that started to put a strain on our marriage. He started to think, is she cheating, or is she staying in the church? So, we would fight to the point where we would actually physically fight, like punches, and horrible words. Then we'd go back and serve in the ministry.

It was hypocritical. I couldn't live like that. I can't go and sing, whether it's a concert or worship service. I can't pretend to be something that I'm not. So that was really eating at me. Then he was really upset because he felt like I was putting it [the church] before him. There has to be a balance again, even with church. You don't need to be in the church building seven days a week. That doesn't make you a better Christian, because then, if your house is not clean and that's causing stress in your marriage, or if you're never home so your husband's drinking more, and then you come home and you're mad that he's drinking—then you guys are fighting. I mean, it's a vicious cycle. You have to find a healthy balance and we were not. So that started to put a stress on our marriage. It was really bad.

Mari says her marriage wasn't the only thing going bad. Her beloved church took a turn for the worse. "They started out with good intentions. They were about their Father's business. But by the end of the twelve years, it turned into their own business. It was the hardest thing I ever had to do [leave the church], because I never wanted to leave there. It became cultish, and I was only using my gift for them. They threatened when I left that I was never going to make it."

Still, there was a bright spot that came during her time at that church—Mari became a mom. "I didn't want to get pregnant, but I wasn't upset that I was either. I was scared for my health and to have the baby. I ended up being right, because I honestly did have a really hard labor. I was in ICU for thirty days. I didn't get to see my baby. I got an infection in my blood. They didn't think I was going to make it, and it ended up being traumatic." But the trauma didn't stop her from being aware of her new purpose as a mom:

> This is my assignment. Now I have to take care of this child. Meanwhile, I'm in church all the time and also thinking, am I going to be like her [my biological mom] or not because this is when it's going to happen. I think I over-thought it so much that I actually withdrew.

> Even when I got home from the hospital, I used that I was ill as an excuse. But it was actually that I was worried that I wouldn't be a good mom. I let my husband's mother bathe the baby at first. I wouldn't bathe her. I wouldn't really touch her or anything. I was so scared of failing, so scared of being like Maureen, my biological mother, that I just wasn't a good mom at first. I wasn't present really. I kind of hid myself away, and that wasn't fair, because those moments go by so fast, those first few months.

Terrified that she'd mother just like her biological mom, Mari hid in the shadows. Fear and avoidance were constant companions. Daily she offered excuses to stay away from her child. She would plead lingering illness, difficulties from her

C-section or trouble with breastfeeding, just to keep herself from "hurting" her baby:

> I still tried to feed the baby, but I didn't want to end up giving her the antibiotics (in her breastmilk) either, so I didn't get that bonding too much, because, literally, I could only do ten days of breastfeeding. I was upset at myself for that, because I was like, I'm already not good, I'm already failing. And it's like, no, you're trying. You've got to give yourself a pat on the back that you're doing that. But you don't see it until after. So, any mom that's going through that now, seriously, it's okay. Don't worry about it. If you can just hold them and give them the bottle, it's that bonding moment.

Finally, Mari found her bonding moment in the water of a warm bath. The moment began when Mari asked her mother-in-law if she could have a hand at bathing her baby. "'Lupe, let me try to do this for my child.' When her little face looked up at me and smiled, I was like, wow, I'm your mom. I can do this, and I want you to know I love you so much, I'm not going to hurt you."

In that moment, Mari started to become the mom she wanted to be, a mom who was completely different from the mother she feared she'd be.

Recalling this breakthrough brings Mari to tears. "That really changed a lot for me, just to see her little face. She was so brown and so cute. That changed everything that day." But Mari admits she still battled mothering insecurities:

I started to put her in the stroller myself and take her out for a walk. I remember the first time I took her out. It was still winter, and I put her in the stroller. I wrapped her up really well and I did my best. Then when I took her out, you know those old-school strollers, when you have to detach them and everything. So, I took it out, and she came tumbling out, thankfully on top of the blanket. But the blanket unrolled, and this little face is looking up at me like, Oh my God.

It's funny today, but I remember that day freaking out. I'm the worst mother in the world. I just dropped my baby in the snow. Things are going to keep happening to try to make you think that, and you have to be like, no, it's just trial and error. There's no perfect recipe.

Instinctively, Mari is aware that many moms battle insecurity and succumb to negative self-talk about their own mothering. "Stop it," Mari scolds. "If you love someone, you keep trying. And that's my biggest hurdle. As I would wash her hair and brush her hair, I would remember what was done to me, and I'd be so gentle. I love her so much. I would see the opposite effect, that she would then want to hug me. She would come running to me as she got older and would love me and then I was like, wow, I am doing something right here."

Mari had a life-changing realization that she was a loving mom even though her own mom was not. She makes the argument that "bad mothering" can actually help us learn good mothering. If you think about it, negative mothering experiences remind us of the enormous impact every mom can have—for harm or for good.

Linda seconds this thought with her own brand of cheering on moms, "I just see these moms at the playground and they don't think they're doing a great job. I just tell them, 'you're here, you're watching out for their safety.'" She says she takes every opportunity she can to encourage moms.

The power that every mom holds makes me realize there's no such thing as "an average mom." Perhaps you feel average, like you're nothing special as a mom. Maybe you think you're not moving mountains or changing the world. Or you think your mothering couldn't possibly have a big impact because you're not seeing any big results. Maybe you don't think your daily sacrifice is showing up in your child's behavior. Maybe you feel like your mom job isn't important because it's not honored by your family. Or esteemed by our culture.

There is no such thing as "an average mom."

But your mothering job is important and Mari's story proves it. She can tell you about the titanic impact bad mothering had on her life before she was rescued by good mothering. She knows personally the huge reverberations of a mother's treatment. When done poorly, it can rob a life of its potential. When done well, it can cause a life to prosper.

Mari would tell you that a mom's work is self-perpetuating, negatively or positively, "Right now, you're not seeing the consequences, but keep doing that [abusing], eventually there's going to be consequences. The child is going to grow. They are going to be that person that abuses somebody else. They are going to be that person that's insecure. They are going to be that person that is angry all the time. Or you can love and nurture them, and they're not going to be perfect. No one ever will be, but you'll see a different outcome. You can tell a tree by its fruit. And the apple doesn't fall far from the tree."

Of course, Mari was an apple that did fall far from its tree. Her story is one of overcoming only because other moms stepped in to adopt her as their own. Moms like Linda. Linda proudly observes that "Mari broke the mold" of her bio mom because she was able to mother her daughter without the violence that scarred her own childhood.

Linda declares "our past does not define us" and Mari is living proof because she refused to mother from that familiar place of abuse. Instead, she chose to mother in the style modeled by her step-in moms.

In addition to her adoptive mom Linda, Mari gives credit to her mother-in-law, Lupe, who stepped up as mother and grandmother. Mari says Lupe gently modeled how to care for her little girl. "Lupe would teach me how to wrap her; she's like 'la viento,' the wind, cannot touch her back at all. Then wrap it like it was the perfect, precious little gift. It didn't have to be a fancy blanket. So, I would do that with my daughter, taking on that culture. Even if I only just have this rice and beans for you today, I'm going to make it the best way possible for you. It is just taking what I have and doing the best I can with it."

Mari openly shares the love she has for her Latin heritage and its influence on her motherhood and family life. She glows about the family principles passed down to her:

> Because family is everything to them, they don't need material things. When you're in a Latin home, if you have one apple and there are twelve people in the room, you're going to slice it to make sure it feeds twelve people. It's not about who can get "up" on one person. It's all about how can I help my

brother, how can I help my sister? I'm going to make sure that I get a company, so I can have my family work for me.

It's all about family. You give your life, literally. They would take a bullet for family members. Also, what I admire is they don't show when there are problems. You could be on the streets tomorrow, [but] that kid is going to think that everything is okay. You're going to be okay because you're so loved and protected.

Mari now works to instill these same values and habits in her daughter Michael. "I'm so excited to be a mom to the most beautiful little girl, and I know all moms say that, but I can't help it." With Michael in her teens, Mari wants to model healthy motherhood for her daughter, so Mari now chooses to put her husband and daughter ahead of her career:

I just went on the road and I took her with me. She's actually so helpful. Now I just teach her, so I actually had to go to her school and speak with her teachers, because she misses some stuff, so we have to find a balance. This year we're going to have to decide whether she's going to be completely homeschooled.

Trying to find that balance is not too hard with her, but finding the balance with my husband was hard, because he is a contractor and he has to be here in the city. It's more still making sure that he is not just alone, because he misses us both. I won't see them [her husband and daughter] when I'm on the road. I won't see them when I'm in Tennessee, so I think taking one of my other homes out of the picture would allow me to be with them even more. Because I was gone so much last year in the studio, I'm really, really focusing on my family. But I'm still working on music, because I have the material ready to go.

On the days when she's unable to mother her daughter at home, Mari lives out Yvonne Pointer's principle of mothering others. "Motherhood now is everything to me, because it's not just for my daughter, but I see people all around the world that just need love. And so now I'm a mother on the road, I'm a mother in the grocery store, I'm a mother everywhere. I just feel like I value it so much more, because I'm not that mother that I grew up with." She adds, "I'm so glad that I have a redemption story."

This brings us to Mari's reason, the one I pointed to when we began her story. Mari sings so she can spread the hope of redemption. Redemption from our past. Redemption in our motherhood. Redemption by God's grace.

Redemption is where the story ends for Mari and her biological mom:

> I was sleeping one night and I felt led to get on Facebook... I Googled her and I Facebook messaged her. I couldn't find her on Google. Then I found one of my siblings and they told me where she was. I literally went from Yonkers to a ghetto in Boston, and I picked her up and brought her to where I was. But while I was there with her, that's when I said the prayer with her. The night when she came over, she was such a mess. She looked horrible. She could

barely walk. She couldn't make it to the bathroom in time. She had diarrhea all over my floor. Literally, I can say she's already been punished, so why would I need to stay angry at her? I actually just immediately felt pity on her.

Pity?! Pity for the woman who threatened her with battery acid? Who told her she was fat and ugly? Who stabbed her with a fork? For the woman who completely failed her as a mother? This is the woman, the mom, that Mari finally and fully forgave.

"We have to love and we have to forgive. That doesn't mean that we're not human and we're not going to feel certain ways. I want people to understand you will go through an emotional process. But just know that, at the end, it's better for you to forgive. It's better for your healing to move

We have to love and we have to forgive.

forward. If you hold it in, it's just going to make it worse. You don't want that to fester inside of you, because then it's harder to get rid of later on in life."

Mothering is a redemption story for Mari Burelle. It was in redemption that she discovered new life—as a mother, as a daughter, and as a woman who can be "mom" to anyone who needs one. She has found a mothering secret that must be shared: You DON'T have to repeat the mistakes of your mom. You can rise from the ashes and find beauty—the beauty of mothering well. The lyrics from one of Mari's songs sum it up:

"Fly. This is my moment in time. I am a warrior lifting my battle cry. I stand and deliver. I open my wings up and fly."

From "FLY"
Lyrics by Mari Burelle

Mari's Mothering Secret:

You don't have to repeat your mother's mistakes.

Why **You** Are Amazing #7:
(re-read often)

You are a one-of-a-kind mom. Whether you had a positive or negative upbringing from your own mom, you have the power to mother your own way. You aren't exactly like your mom and that's good.
You have unique gifts that your kids uniquely need.

Chapter 8
Hope In the Goodbye
Kara Tippetts

She has the life story none of us would choose. She got the cancer diagnosis when her youngest child was three. The next two years were full of struggle. That struggle became the subject of a popular documentary. A film that portrayed her decision to live her last years well. For her kids. For her husband. For God. She chose a "hardest peace" that many moms can learn from.

✳✳✳✳✳✳

Lots of people say they want to live as if they might die tomorrow, but Kara was forced to live that way. She knew how precious life was because, as a thirty-six-year-old mom, she confronted death. This is why I yearn to give Kara's story the value—the justice—it deserves, because Kara's life had to be on the line for her to discover her unique mothering secret. And a life is a lot to give in exchange for a secret shared.

I've pondered how to tell Kara Tippetts's story in a way that does her justice. I've realized that I cannot. But Kara's story must be told because it reminds us of what truly matters. Her limited lifetime magnified the urgency of love—including the priceless importance of mother love.

I feel almost desperate to share her love lesson because, in a way, Kara had to die for it to be learned. It was her approaching death that shaped her unique perspective, a daily awareness that our family moments are precious and fragile and not to be wasted.

Kara's life and death offer moms a rare reminder that our sneaky modern-day distractions should NOT be allowed to snuff out our precious mothering moments. Not business emails or troubling texts, not flat tires or fancy Facebook posts, not burned dinners or dirty dishes. This brave woman had the unique outlook of a mom who knew every moment with her children was precious, because her remaining moments were few.

Kara Tippetts's story has leveled me and changed me. When I first came across Kara, I was busy raising my pre-teen girl and teenage boy and I was occupied with running ChannelMom's radio show and nonprofit outreach. I was always looking for good interview subjects among the many pitched to me by book agents and PR people. When I received a pitch to feature Kara's latest book, *The Hardest*

Peace, I gave it a look. Almost immediately her book bore a hole into my heart.

I quickly realized the hardest thing about Kara's search for peace in the midst of terminal cancer was her children. Four kids. Far from being grown up. Far from having the opportunity to be fully raised by their mom. This wrecked me. The idea of leaving my own children before I had the time to raise them was, for me, an excruciating thought. And that's where the change came in. I vowed, in the midst of reading Kara's book, that I would become more dedicated to treasuring the moments, even the difficult ones, with my kids.

It's as if Kara is calling back down the mothering trail with an admonition for each one of us: "Hey, ladies, here it is. This is motherhood, and this is why and how you should treasure it. Because here I am, not knowing if I can finish raising my children before I die."

If I'm honest, I think I'm also motivated by "survivor's guilt." I have survived. Even though I was diagnosed with cancer too, my battle was small compared to Kara's. God allowed me to stay alive at least long enough to raise my children into young adulthood. So, I feel I owe it to Kara to share her secret well because she was never given the chance to live her mothering secret to its fullest.

When I interviewed Kara, she'd already been dealing with various cancer diagnoses for two-and-a-half years. It began with breast cancer, but more recently cancer had been found in her reproductive system and brain. At the time of our interview, Kara's daughter Eleanor was thirteen, her second-born, Harper Joy, was ten. Her only son, Lake Edward, was eight and her "baby," Story Jane, was five. Just typing these ages hurts my heart.

I began the interview by focusing on Kara's writing about mothering her youngest, Story Jane. In her book, she had recounted Story Jane's heart-wrenching habit of tracing her mommy's surgery scars with her little fingers, finding any opportunity to press close to the body that bore those scars:

> Story Jane sees them, asks about them and then lingers closely, knowing only a fraction of what they mean. I think she knows the heart of what my scars represent, but her littleness, like my own so many years ago, makes understanding our developing story difficult. I could not know the heart of my dad and his anger, because of the littleness I watched from. Story also struggles to know and understand the hurt of our story from the perch of young age. She witnesses the tears and sees my baldness, but all she knows is the warmth of my touch here today and the kindness that greets her in her living. She has found new, soft corners next to me that suffice where surgery has left me utterly changed. What she longs for is my closeness, my touch, my kindness to meet her each cold evening when she sneaks quietly into my bed to be near me.
>
> She no longer asks for entrance next to me in the little hours of the night. She quietly enters by my feet and finds the warm curve in my back and returns to the comfort of her dreams next to her mama. Years will give her understanding like they gave me. But today, sitting next to my love is enough. The other day she proclaimed that she never wanted to leave my side, that I was always the warmth she liked best. I said nothing, only snuggled closer with the

hope for more days. More and more days of loving her. I want her to look back and see herself, a daughter loved.

Kara unwraps this deeply personal moment by telling me why she shared it in the book: "I feel like she's trying to multiply her love and time with me in the night as she comes. And, as an exhausted young mom, I would so often meet my kids in the night and think, oh, tomorrow's not going to be as great of a day because my sleep has been interrupted. You know, all of those struggles. And they're real. I mean, sleep deprivation is no joke. It is hard, but yet, now I realize, this is my baby multiplying. She is not going to get as many days as my oldest did. And so, we multiply that in the night, and we love on each other, and I love it, instead of thinking, woe is me, tomorrow is going to be hard."

Enveloped in that bittersweet, midnight moment is Kara's mothering secret—love big. Love BIG. Despite the diagnosis. Despite the difficult circumstances. Despite even the threat of death. Love BIG as a mom. Her secret was born during her hardest days as she committed to actively loving her children despite her life-stealing hardship.

Kara seems aware that her serious situation makes us more likely to take her

These little moments are the big moments of life.

secret seriously. But hold on. Before we go on, I've got to acknowledge that Kara's serious situation was transformed by her serious faith. I'm aware that her "faith talk" in this chapter could cause some moms to tune out.

Not every mother falls in line with a faith like Kara's. Not every mother believes like Kara does. In fact, some moms are turned off by that kind of belief. But Kara's words are for non-believing moms too. Honestly, we can all tune in as she reminds us to treasure our mothering moments and to see our mothering as a high calling:

> You know, just the high and beautiful calling of being a mom. These little moments are the big moments of life. And so often, as moms, we're waiting for the promotion, the next house, the vacation... oh, on vacation, I'll finally rest. And we struggle to live present in our moments with our families. That to me is the high calling of being a mom, of being present, of being available.
>
> You know, so many people say it's quality, not quantity, but I just disagree. In the quantity of all these million moments that we, as moms, get to capture, we find quality. So, it's to be cherished, and our job, our high calling, is to cherish these kids. As our kids are little, we are representative of who Christ is. We are representative of God the Father. Until they take hold of that themselves, we get to be this living picture of a gracious and loving God. It's a high calling and it's so, so, so important.

Kara's faith shines more brightly against the contrasting darkness of her cancer struggle; it's that stark contrast that makes her faith humbling to observe. Despite the fact that Kara had so much to lose at so young an age, she insisted on offering herself up as a life lesson. She was determined to keep her faith intact, just as she was determined to find lessons in dying, so she could pass them on to moms still living:

It was a life-changer when I had my daughter. And before I had her, somebody challenged me to live in kindness. I have always understood and just loved being a mom. But so much of those little moments, I felt like they were to get through. You know, let's get through this infancy stage. Let's get through the hard discipline years. And cancer has taught me just to slow down and say, you know what, all I have is today. That's all I have. I don't have tomorrow. I have today. And, as I pray for more time, I have to realize that each moment I'm given now is an answer to that prayer of more time.

I often struggle, because I wonder, would healthy Kara have listened to sick Kara? And that's the struggle... for all of us. Could my perspective teach us? Could we have teachable hearts to hear that these moments matter and to let it change our hearts, not just change our actions. The gospel says we are united with Christ and, in that union from the overflow of Jesus' love, we get to overflow and spill out this love, this generous love that is given to us.

There it is again, Kara's mothering secret. Keep finding ways to love, no matter what your circumstances are, no matter what level of faith you have. Love your children. Love your spouse. Love your neighbors. Love. BIG.

Kara's dedicated approach to being a loving parent could be a direct response to the hurtful parenting she received from her own father. In *The Hardest Peace*, she revealed one example of that pain:

It starts as a child. I'm wrapped in fear, afraid my timid bladder will spill on the brown, shag carpet. Staring at the beet-red face from little eyes, little body, little everything, the enormity of my father's anger is too big for me. He sees me struggling to hold my urine inside. He sees me weakening under his bellowing anger. I am sent to retrieve the paddle from the wall. His paddle is always used. He's always the one to deliver the verdict. Always show me my failures. Always remind me of my faults.

I tremble under the weight of his anger. I can feel my pee coming. I return with the paddle and the brotherhood delivers my judgment. [She refers to the brotherhood, because it's a paddle from his days as a fraternity member.] I crumple under the pain. It pales in comparison to his screaming. The pain of the paddle isn't nearly the pain of a daddy screaming at you. The pain came with the harsh and angry words, not the paddle. I am released first to the bathroom and then the quiet of my room to change my soiled clothes.

Like so many of us, Kara struggled with hurtful memories of childhood pain. As a teenager, she looked for ways to shut out the pain however she could. "You know, I think it's a numbing to pain... in the brokenness of relationships within my family. I had no way. I had no tools. I had no emotional maturity, spiritual maturity. I didn't even have the ability to communicate the brokenness that I felt. My reaction was to numb my life and run, simply run, and create family with girlfriends, create family anywhere but within my home, and run."

Kara's not afraid to unveil her rebellious behavior during those days of "running." She doesn't pretend to have been a good, little Christian her whole life. In fact, she's brutally honest in all the best ways. I believe her honesty might allow others who've also "run" away in their lives to feel understood and accepted. I admire Kara for revealing her own bad behavior in her book and I say to her:

> You admit that kind of a childhood led you to rebellion. And it was so great to hear you talk about your beer-drinking, pot-smoking, boy-pursuing days, because so many millions of teenagers are in that place. They're mad about their own childhood pain, whatever it may be, and they use it as an excuse to drink a bunch of beer and smoke pot and party. And I'll tell you what, I think a lot of us have been there. I was there for a while. We've all been in that kind of immature, "let's go party to make ourselves feel better" place. And so, you talk about that, and it's an incredible thing for you to be able to reveal that. I was seeing so many people in your description there, and I thought, oh my gosh, this is just every teenager that is rebelling in some form. She's describing it and I'm so glad she is.

Kara admits the rebellion was a turning point for her because it didn't work. It didn't heal her pain. It didn't fix her life. It was a dead-end path to an empty soul. "And so, when somebody presented me the truth of the life, death and resurrection of Jesus, I immediately saw it as true, and I saw it as something I needed. And God plucked me from that dark place and brought me to Himself. It was life-altering.

I mean, I was a different person. And it was hard. I mean, here I had created this community with my partying friends, and all at once I'm saying, wait, I think I want to live differently. It was a lonely time. It was a hard time, but it was also just rich. Rich in understanding forgiveness. It was beautiful."

"Beautiful" eventually translated into something bigger for Kara. Her newfound faith led her not only to an understanding that Christ forgave it all, but also to a transformational decision to forgive her father. She was able to let go of years of rage and abuse at the hands of her father:

> *Foregiveness is really a gift we give ourselves.*

You know, the journey for me was a brokenness in my relationship with my father that then led to my rebellion. And in my rebellion is when I came to Christ. So, for me, it's the beautiful story of brokenness that led me to Jesus. And though it hurts, and even hearing you re-read some of that brings heartache, that was the journey planned for me and that was the place where I was drawn to Christ. And, in that, not just forgiveness for myself—because I own a lot of my own rebellion in that chapter—but forgiveness towards my dad, who just simply did not have tools and didn't have a faith that my husband and I have now.

My hope in it is there [are] so many people who live so tied in unforgiveness from a painful childhood and it's stunting. It stunts our growth. Forgiveness is really a gift we give ourselves. It's not something that has been ever asked of me from my father, but yet, as I grow older and realize how hard living is, how stressful finances, how stressful marriage and parenting really [are], I can see a gracious place for my father where he didn't have faith, he didn't have a community. And he really lived a hidden life behind closed doors and taught us all to live a very hidden life. You know, we had our public persona and then we had the life we lived behind closed doors. And I think that's the story of so many of us. We live two very different lives, behind closed doors and in public... we're on social media. And I think God wants us to live an authentic life, both places.

As Kara refers to the hidden lives many of us live, often hiding our true lives on social media or at cocktail parties, I ask her to be "real" about her true self. "What do you want people to know about you that is misunderstood when we say, 'She's got cancer and she wrote a book.' What do you want people to know today about you, that will do some good?"

Kara says, "I write about my journey and the hard edges of life that have met me in a way that isn't simply about cancer. It's about how all of us meet the places of life we didn't expect. Marriage may be not what we expected. Parenting, maybe we realize we're more angry than we ever realized. Life throws these curve balls at us... and in those places, so often we feel like we've made a mistake or we're doing something wrong. How come my life isn't 'Pinteresty' like everybody else?"

There's that social media reference again, an issue many moms struggle with, as they compare their mom lives to other mom lives on social media. People (including me) tend to put out their best moments, their best photos, their best "stuff" on Facebook, Instagram and Pinterest. And then, many of us mamas tend to compare our personal "worst" with the "best" of others that we see on social media.

I lament about that comparison game to Kara: "I think social media has been devastating, because we're all throwing up our pictures of margaritas in Mexico, and no one's saying, 'oh, by the way, I'm completely depressed today because of something my son said to me or because I'm battling an illness or because my marriage is a mess,' or whatever it is. I mean, who's posting that on Facebook?"

Speaking from my own personal experience, I admit I've often found myself feeling worse, not better, after perusing Facebook, casually noting which friends obviously have nicer homes, better vacations, more impressive careers... and, yes, bigger diamonds. Yuck! What's wrong with me for failing to want the best for my old high school or college friends? As a "good Christian," I should just be happy for them, but instead, I find myself feeling bad about my life in comparison to theirs.

In fact, researchers have discovered a developing syndrome of depression and anxiety caused by social media. The syndrome arises when folks compare their real lives to others' Facebook lives (one of my mom friends calls it "Fakebook"). In addition to that, social media depression can come from failing to have real interactions with real people. Kara points out that, when online comparison and isolation make us feel "less than" everyone else, we tend to hide ourselves and our suffering:

> And, in that place, we hide. Shame and fear keep us hidden in our grievances. And I think, with my story, I put it out there and say, "Suffering is not a mistake.

These are the places that God has made me needy for Him, and how can that be a mistake?"

And so, that is my message to anyone. It's not just a story of cancer, but when we meet those disappointments in life, how do we also meet our neediness of God and community and walk in that, walk in community and limp along and pull each other towards Jesus? It's not simply another cancer story, though that is the edge of life that God has used to draw me to Himself. But we all, all of us, especially as mothers, face it and hide and compete and struggle with living in an authentic community.

Speaking to a community of moms was part of Kara's passion. She made a specific decision to share her cancer story—through her blog, books, interviews and, eventually, through a documentary about her life, *The Long Goodbye: The Kara Tippetts Story*. The publications and productions gave Kara the chance to say, "Here's what I'm learning," and to ask, "How can I help you in the midst of your battles?" She made it clear that the battle doesn't have to be cancer. It also doesn't have to be a quote-unquote death sentence. It can be a marriage struggle, a work struggle or a raising-the-kids struggle; whatever it is, Kara's heart was to help women gain a new perspective about God and purpose and what really matters in the midst of our mama struggles.

Love is what matters most. In. Every. Moment.

The reality check that cancer gave Kara was that love is what matters most. In. Every. Moment. Of course, we can enjoy the big, eventful moments, but we shouldn't overlook the poignant possibilities contained in our "smallest" moments. In Kara's words: "I mean, just to obviously enjoy the big moments and the celebratory events, but to also just embrace the little moments, sitting face-to-face, looking at each other at the dinner table and say[ing], 'Who brought you joy today? How did you share Jesus to somebody else today? How's your heart doing today?' And see those moments as just as important as the giant moments."

Like many American moms—busy impressing, accomplishing, checking off lists—I get stuck in the accomplishment questions: When's the next big breakthrough? When's the next promotion? When will our finances be secure? When will we get new kitchen counters? When will my child behave the way I've been training him to behave? But Kara reminds me that we can't squander all the little moments by waiting for what we define as big moments. The little moments are rich with importance. That's a lesson I need to remember.

I feel like these little lessons Kara shares, just months before saying goodbye to life with her family, are pregnant with urgency for us. An urgency to learn from her. I find myself wanting to plead with every mom to learn from dying Kara. I don't want her battle with cancer to be a waste. I have a hope that, in the moment she came face to face with God, she was able to say with satisfaction, "So many people were blessed and helped by my hard story." I have a hope that this might have been the moment that made Kara's unfinished mothering business finally have a purpose.

I bawled over Kara's lessons in dying because of how death was pressing in on her, suffocating her with the force of a dreaded goodbye. Saying goodbye to her very young children. I've yearned to share her love lessons with every mother in the world. I want every mother, including myself, to have the benefit of Kara's perspective—that choosing love and joy and peace and forgiveness is always possible if we imagine dying tomorrow. That's what Kara was forced to do, and she was a better mother for it.

Kara's limited time taught her to LOVE like many of us never do. Her fading life unveiled a kind of desperate "need to love," which was formerly muddied by the busyness of daily living. Her recognition gave birth to her steadfast commitment to love her own kids well. And to pass this love lesson on to other moms who did not have the sobering perspective of fast-approaching death.

The day I interviewed Kara my best friend Shelley was in the radio studio with me. Shelley shared an observation with Kara, which I now see as a wake-up call for every mom. Here's how Shelley put it. "My thought is that all of us really have a death sentence, if that's the way we want to put it. I know many people who have cancer are given this many months to live, something like that, but we all really only have so much time to live. Those of us who haven't been told by our doctors, with all their infinite knowledge, don't have that sentence put out for us, but really, we all have that sentence. For Jenny and I, it could be tonight on our way home."

Kara immediately agrees. "I think it's absolutely true. You know, I say that my kids are afforded to me the long goodbye... and it has built a conversation about heaven that wasn't previously present in our home. And I think you're right. I mean, obviously it's not natural. We weren't originally made to die, but it's inevitable. We now all die, but we don't die a death that is forever when we are united with Christ. And so, you're absolutely right. I think [with] my cancer, God has used it to say exactly what you just said—to all of us. None of us are promised tomorrow.

We have this breath and are we going to live this breath well?

I thank Kara for this question. It's a question I need to recite daily as a mom. Am I going to live this breath well? Am I going to teach my kids to live their breaths well? It's a minute-by-minute choice.

I ask Kara if she ever resents the people who tell her to keep her chin up or to look on the bright side. I even venture to ask a more sensitive question. Does she struggle with the scriptures that promise God's good for her life? I read Psalm 84: 5-6 (HCSB) out loud to her: "Happy are the people whose strength is in You, whose hearts are set on a pilgrimage. As they pass through the valley of Baca [which can also mean tears], they make it a source of spring water. Even the autumn rain will cover it with blessings." I ask Kara if she resents Psalms like that, suggesting it all works out in the end. She responds with a quiet "No, no," and explains:

> You know, I read about David today, and I don't know if that particular one was written by David, but he was this dancing king that found joy even in the midst of heartache. And I want to be like him... but so often, you know, I have to fight for that peace in the sorrow. And when I forget, I have this beautiful community that gathers around me and reminds me. And so, you know, God has kept me from anger. And Jason, my husband, and I have fought for tender hearts through this. And it is a battle.
>
> I often say I'm a woman whose story has been shattered into a million pieces, but each of those million pieces is known and kept. And so, in that place, how could there be bitterness? Why would I

choose that? Because, you know, the hard thing for me, and I think for all of us, we see, feel, hear, touch this place, and we struggle to have an imagination for the next. But each day I suffer, I grow in a longing for heaven and to be with Jesus and just to dance with Him and enjoy Him forever.

Kara seems to taste the peace that comes from the promise of Heaven, but she confesses that the needs of life on earth still kick in.

I think I enjoy a lot of peace, and yet there is an intensity that comes with a terminal illness that makes every moment feel so big, and sometimes that can be daunting.

Sometimes, you know, I get jealous. I saw a woman with beautiful highlights, and I felt jealous that she could just leisurely sit in a chair and get highlights [laughs]. You know, sometimes I just long for some normality, and yet, this is the story I've been asked to receive.

And that's just a small part of what makes Kara's peace hard—like the title of her book, *The Hardest Peace*. I ask Kara what the hardest peace actually is. "That's a great question. My editor's wife one night said to him, 'The hardest piece for me is that Kara has young children.' And he turned to her and goes, 'The hardest piece?' And he came, and we started talking and imagining this book. What if we

What if suffering isn't a mistake?

talked about the hard journey in knowing God's peace in the midst of suffering?"

It was then that Kara decided to utilize the play on words, and she moved from discussing the hardest "piece" into the hardest "peace." Kara explains,

> I think so much about our culture, so much about even our Christian culture, is so bent on winning and so bent on performance and [being] happy that I bring a different story. What if suffering isn't a mistake? What if our brokenness is the most beautiful part of each of our stories? And what if seeking God's peace in our neediness and desperate places is beautiful? And so, the hardest peace is this journey, in the brokenness of my story, to knowing God's nearness is my only good. It is my only good.

Wow. Are any of us able to do what Kara has done? To find "good" in our suffering? To believe the good in our suffering is intended to be for us? I think if we really worked to view suffering this way, there would be more contentment in our lives. This is much easier said than done, but the idea of "good contained in suffering" makes me think of Michele Cushatt (Chapter 6). Michele battled through tongue cancer THREE times, finally having two-thirds of her tongue removed and rebuilt by cutting flesh out of other parts of her body, all while undergoing chemo and radiation on her head. Michele said she couldn't even fully describe how horrific her suffering was; however, she says she would not wish to have avoided that suffering, because of the good it brought her.

What if we took a cue from Kara and Michele? What if, in the midst of our suffering or difficulties, we believed that good would come? Would that radically change the trajectory of our lives? Would it transform us into more joy-filled mamas? Would it be a life-changing lesson that we could model for our kids so they would benefit? Yes, yes, yes, yes, yes...

Kara did find the good in suffering. She even dared to call it "beautiful." She pointed out that cancer had turned her entire family toward a conversation about Heaven. And it allowed her to have a long goodbye with her children that many moms never experience. "When we started, it was [ages] eleven to three and one of my big hopes was that my daughter, my youngest, would be old enough that she would have her own memories of me and not have to inherit them from her older siblings, though they would give them to her. But you know, I remember being five and so, for me, that is such a grace that God has given me these two years, and he's given me today, so I get to keep living them with all my children and my husband."

When Kara is able to see grace in extra days of mothering her kids, I'm almost ashamed. I think of how I overlook grace on days when I'm stressed because I'm rushing and I'm going to be late (again). Or I'm angry because of something I read in an email. Or I'm upset because my house doesn't look as impressive as my friend's house. Or I'm mad because someone cut me off in traffic. Or the blow dryer stopped working. Or my husband forgot to kiss me goodbye. Whatever! What's my problem?!! Daily, I need to let Kara's memory remind me of the beauty and grace in just being able to love my children. That's it. Full stop.

I need to practice love. All moms do. It might be very difficult when babies are crying through the night or toddlers are coloring on the walls or teenagers are rebelling with drugs. It might seem nearly impossible in the midst of postpartum depression or a husband having an affair or a health crisis that creates financial devastation. It might be hard, like Kara's peace was hard. But, with God, it's not impossible.

Kara's love lesson can be carried on through our practices as moms. Together, moms, we can pray for love and forgiveness to come. We can hang up sayings or scriptures throughout our homes, reminding us (and our children) to choose love. We can create a daily mantra that directs us back to the love we know we *want* to give, even on the hardest days. Here's a saying we can all speak out loud together: "God, help me to love, because you love me." I know the instinct of almost every mom is to love. So, it's going to feel better if you just let that instinct live.

In the end, it was through Kara's suffering and death that God amplified her mothering call to love big. Love. Big. That's all.

Let's vow to live out Kara's lesson with the somber recognition that it was through her death that Kara had the opportunity to share her most important mothering secret with every mom who needs it. Kara can no longer love BIG in the presence of children. But we still can, so love BIG, mom. Because you can.

Kara's Mothering Secret:
Love BIG.

Why **You** Are Amazing #8
(re-read often)

You love your kids. And boy do they need it.
Every. Single. Day.
The power of a mother is the power of love.
Is there anything better? Your love is made in
the glorious image of the God who loves them.

EPILOGUE: A Last Word for Moms

I hope this book has encouraged you. I hope you see the calling of motherhood in a brand new light. And I hope that light has fully illuminated your immeasurable value as the mother of your children.

I also hope you now see that your mothering impacts the future of our world, for better or for worse. May this book inspire you to keep choosing "better." Mother well, my mom friends. The whole world will benefit when you do.

And, one more hope: I hope that your mom life will be changed in the best ways, now that you're armed with eight secrets shared by the moms in this book.

May you be empowered by Amazing Mom Secret #1: **Believe that being a mom is incredibly important.** Your importance is inherent in the power you have to change the world by the way you raise your children.

May you be emboldened by Amazing Mom Secret #2: **Make a positive difference in response to your pain** because you will have pain and you can use it to make the world a better place. And you can teach your kids how to do the same.

May you be a difference-maker through Amazing Mom Secret #3: **Overcome social media negativity by teaching your kids kindness, honesty and respect.** Arm your kids with these character traits, and they'll be equipped to respond positively to the negative universe of social media.

May you be challenged by Amazing Mom Secret #4: **Make your kids a top priority.** You have the unique potential to make your kids feel valued, just by showing up. Sacrificing status, material things, and even self, will help your kids feel loved, as they see you making them a priority.

May you be assured you're enough through Amazing Mom Secret #5: **Give yourself a break because no woman can have it all.** Refuse to feel guilt when you realize you don't have what another mom has. You don't need to have it all to be a good mom.

May you be inspired by Amazing Mom Secret #6: **Disciple your babies. Teach them about the love of God.** Lead your children in the way of gracious love that comes from God. There is no negative in telling your children that God loves them.

May you be an overcomer with Amazing Mom Secret #7: **Know that you don't have to repeat your mom's mistakes.** Stop living in fear that you'll make the same hurtful mistakes that your mom (or dad) made. You can parent differently. It's also a good idea to forgive the flaws of your parents, just as you'll want your kids to forgive you one day.

And may you be motivated to love even more from Amazing Mom Secret #8: **Love BIG.** What else can I say? Love is the primary thing in parenting. It lies behind all of the other secrets.

At the end of this book is a handy list of all eight secrets, summarized, made just for you—rip it out and tape it to your fridge or take a picture and post it somewhere—to keep these "amazing mom secrets" front and center.

And now I want to offer a few last words of encouragement to place an exclamation point on your value as an utterly unique and amazing mom.

I believe God specifically designed women for this most important role of motherhood. I believe He has you carry that baby inside of you for nine months so you have an immediate and inherent investment in that little one. A physical bond is literally enforced.

You are invited to join God in the creation process or He chooses the specific children you were meant to adopt. I've been amazed at how fine-tuned the matching process is for my friends who adopt—right down to how their "forever children" look like them. Of course, when it comes to fostering, I deeply respect and admire the mamas who choose to step into a difficult process after their baby was birthed by another. This is a brave and unselfish decision.

Further, I suspect God created nursing so the bond will continue, although I know it doesn't work for every woman. Feeding your baby from your actual self, in more ways than one, is a beautiful illustration of how much your child depends on you for his or her future development. And it doesn't have to be just feeding by nursing. It can be other kinds of sustenance—a bottle or a song or some cooing or cuddling.

I've even speculated that God made the female figure "softer," because that's a comfort to the children they hold. I'm not suggesting women can't be muscular or that the strength of a dad isn't comforting. I'm just pointing out the specifically designed structure of a mom.

Some of our most important historical figures have also recognized the value of moms. American presidents have often credited their moms for their skill in leading the nation. Our first president, George Washington, is cited as saying, "My mother was the most beautiful woman I ever saw. All I am I owe to my mother. I attribute all my success in life to the moral, intellectual and physical education I received from her."

Abraham Lincoln offered a similar tribute. "All that I am, or hope to be, I owe to my angel mother."

And Barack Obama is quoted as saying: "Mothers are the rocks of our families and a foundation in our communities. In gratitude for their generous love, patient counsel, and lifelong support, let us pay respect to the women who carry out the hard work of motherhood with skill and grace..."

In scripture, Mary was called "blessed among women," because she was chosen to be the mother of Jesus. She was chosen to be the one who would raise Him up to save the world. Not His disciples. Not one of His friends. His mom.

We also know that Jesus so honored his own mom that He made sure someone would care for her after He died. One of the last things Jesus did on earth was assign John to act as his mother's new "son" in order to support her. "Standing near the cross were Jesus' mother, and his mother's sister, Mary... and Mary Magdalene. When Jesus saw his mother standing there beside the disciple he loved, he said to her, 'Dear woman, here is your son.' And he said to this disciple, 'Here is your mother.' And from then on this disciple took her into his home" (John 19: 25-27, NLT).

Jesus knew the value of a mother. He knew that value should be preserved. In fact, God Himself promises to take care of the mothers and their children, using the illustration of mother sheep. "He will feed his flock like a shepherd. He will carry the lambs in his arms, holding them close to his heart. He will gently lead the mother sheep with their yo ung" (Isaiah 40:11, NLT).

Of course, scripture also points to the inherent value of both mothers and fathers. "Honor your father and your mother" (Exodus 20:12).

Finally, the book of Isaiah points to the priceless love and comfort of a mother as it is exhibited by the God of the universe: "As a mother comforts her child, so will I comfort you" (Isaiah 66:13).

When you mother well, multitudes benefit. Not only your children, but you, your spouse, your extended family, your friends, your acquaintances and the world at large. One mom, mothering well, is changing the world. For the better.

So, thank you for being "just a mom"—and so much more.

May God bless each and every one of you.

Endnotes

Preface
1. Darrow L. Miller, *Nurturing The Nations: Reclaiming the Dignity of Women in Building Healthy Cultures,* (Colorado Springs, Paternoster Publishing, 2007) 259-60
2. Julie Roys, *Redeeming the Feminine Soul: God's Surprising Vision for Womanhood* (Nashville, Nelson Books: An Imprint of Thomas Nelson, 2017), 101

Chapter 1
1. Julie Roys, *Redeeming the Feminine Soul: God's Surprising Vision for Womanhood* (Nashville, Nelson Books: an imprint of Thomas Nelson, 2017), 150-151
2. Joseph M. Scriven, *What a Friend We Have in Jesus,* originally written as a poem, 1855; Charles Crozat Converse composed tune for hymn, 1868

Chapter 2
1. John Caniglia and Marvin Fong, "Hernandez Warren's Confession: 'I killed' 14-year-old Gloria Pointer" (cleveland.com and The Plain Dealer, Updated Jan. 12, 2019; Posted April 15, 2014)
2. John Caniglia and Marvin Fong, "Hernandez Warren's Confession: 'I killed' 14-year-old Gloria Pointer" (cleveland.com and The Plain

Dealer, Updated Jan. 12, 2019; Posted April
15, 2014)

Chapter 3
1. Steven Ruiz, "'The Bachelorette' Finale
   Recap: Did Becca Choose the Wrong Guy?"
   (USA Today online, ftw.usatoday.com, Aug. 7,
   2018, USA Today Sports)
2. Darlene Cunha, "I'm One of the 56% of
   American Mothers Who 'Prefer' To Stay
   Home," (TIME Online, Oct. 9, 2015)
3. Mayo Clinic Staff, "Teens and social media
   use: What's the impact?" (mayoclinic.org,
   Dec. 21, 2019)

Chapter 4
1. Institute for Family Studies, IFstudies.org,
   Dec.18, 2017,
2. Sylvia Ann Hewlett and Cornel West, *The War
   Against Parents: What Can We Do For
   America's Beleaguered Moms and Dads* (New
   York, Mariner Books, Houghton Mifflin
   Company, 1998), 40, 164-165
   Wayne Parker, "Statistics on Fatherless
   Children in America," liveabout.com, May 24,
   2019
3. Hewlett and West, *The War Against Parents,*
   164

Chapter 5
1. Julie Roys, *Redeeming the Feminine Soul: God's
   Surprising Vision for Womanhood* (Nashville,

Nelson Books: an imprint of Thomas Nelson, 2017), 91, 151
2. Darlena Cunha, "I'm One of the 56% of American Mothers Who 'Prefer' To Stay Home," (TIME Online, Oct. 9, 2015)
3. Erin Zammett Ruddy, "The Mommy Wars," (Parenting.com)
4. An act which voids forced arbitration agreements that prevent sexual harassment survivors from getting their day in court.

Chapter 8
1. Kara Tippetts, *The Hardest Peace: Expecting Grace in the Midst of Life's Hard,* Kindle version (Colorado Springs, David C. Cook, 2014) 33
2. Kara Tippetts, *The Hardest Peace: Expecting Grace in the Midst of Life's Hard,* Kindle version (Colorado Springs, David C. Cook, 2014) 22

Epilogue
Facebook post, Barack Obama's Facebook page, May 8, 2011

♡Amazing Mom Secrets ♡
For Amazing Moms

- Believe that being a mom is incredibly important.
- Make a positive difference in response to your pain.
- Teach your kids kindness and respect.
- Make your kids a top priority.
- Give yourself a break because no woman has it all.
- Disciple your babies. Teach them about God's love.
- You don't have to repeat your mom's mistakes.
- Love BIG

Made in the USA
Middletown, DE
06 April 2022

63684702R00130